STAND FAST IN FAITH

STAND FAST IN FAITH

FINDING FREEDOM THROUGH DISCIPLINE IN THE TEN COMMANDMENTS

WALLACE E. FISHER

Abingdon
Nashville

STAND FAST IN FAITH

Copyright © 1978 by Abingdon

Library of Congress Cataloging in Publication Data

Fisher, Wallace E.
    Stand fast in faith.

    1. Commandments, Ten. 2.   Christian life—Lutheran
authors. I. Title.
BV4655.F47   241.5′2   77-13284

ISBN 0-687-39271-3

MANUFACTURED BY THE PARTHENON PRESS AT
NASHVILLE, TENNESSEE, UNITED STATES OF AMERICA

For my wife
Margaret Elizabeth

She is of so free, so kind, so apt, so blessed a disposition, she holds it a vice in her goodness not to do more than she is requested.

(*Othello,* act 2, scene 3)

ACKNOWLEDGMENTS

The problem of getting freedom and discipline into balance in individuals' lives—socially, politically, personally—began to focus for me shortly after World War II. These essays, integrally related, represent my present understanding of and response to this crucial problem. The content is informed by my contacts with countless insightful and concerned persons over three decades, beginning with my biblical and theological training at the Lutheran School of Theology at Philadelphia and the sharpened sense of history fostered in the graduate schools of history at the Universities of Pennsylvania and Pittsburgh. My growth in experience, reflection, and study during five years in a college community as a professor-preacher-counselor (1947–52), a quarter of a century as a preacher-counselor-teacher in a large urban church (1952–), and the last two decades as an author-lecturer ranging far beyond my parish, build upon that broad foundation. My debt is wide and deep. I cannot acknowledge it adequately or express fully my gratitude to thousands of people in the States, Canada, and Western Europe who have enriched my thinking and my person.

But I can identify those who helped directly with this book. My secretary, Arline S. Fellenbaum, deserves thanks for preparing the manuscript, helped by Patricia Baker and Dorothy Frank, office secretaries at Trinity Church. I thank especially those who, although burdened with professional and business responsibilities, read the manuscript and offered valuable comments: Cynthia J. Bolbach, Emory Stevens Bucke, Charles F. Drawdy, Craig Dyer, Hugo Eskildson, R. Ray Evelan, Gabriel Fackre, Paul Mark and Elizabeth Anne Fisher, Donald R. Heiges, Earl R. Henley, Jack R. Hoffman, B. Penrose Hoover, Larry L. Lehman, Ann Haagen Musselman, Neale E. Nelson, Donald R. Pichaske, David Rees, Lawrence M. Reese, John and Dorothea Robinson, Hugo W. Schroeder, Jr., Lloyd E. Sheneman, Priscilla Shoup, Harald S. Sigmar, Albert P. Stauderman, William H. Stotler, Edward F. Weiskotten, Kirk and Ann Louise White, William E. Whitesell, and Robert H. Witmer.

My wife, Margaret Elizabeth, who has read critically and often the emerging manuscripts of nine books—and has shared gallantly in my whole ministry—knows my debt to her. The dedication points up one facet of her gracious, resilient, durable person. She is God's best human gift to me.

Wallace E. Fisher
Lancaster, Pennsylvania

CONTENTS

PREFACE

Over the last fifty years, time-honored values of Western society have been wiped out or transmuted beyond recognition. Old and respected guideposts have been swept away. People have given allegiance to false gods, subscribed to inhumane philosophies, been mesmerized by illusion-making psychologies, and have turned to the occult for help. The results of these conscious and unconscious flights from personal and social reponsibility have disabled persons and disrupted society. Psychologist David Schon judges "that in the central aspects of our lives our sense of personal constancy is collapsing and our social stability is going to pieces."

The plea of this book is that we face up to this awesome loss of moral constancy in the Western world: by church people from a biblical perspective and by others (especially parents, educators, and public officials) from a basic moral perspective. The Ten Commandments are employed here as the foundation for the beginnings of this reappraisal in the church as well as the world. Viewed in biblical perspective, the Ten Commandments are devised, not primarily to police people, but to persuade them that they need God and to correct, enlighten, and guide them for responsible living in society.

They are, as the Puritans claimed, "commands with promise."

Christians, serious about following Christ, will recall that Jesus, addressing the religious leaders of his day, said: "If you believed Moses, you would believe what I tell you, for it was about me that he wrote. But if you do not believe what he wrote, how are you to believe what I say?" (John 5:46-47 NEB). The law, together with the prophets, provides much of the religious and social context in which we must understand Jesus. The Commandments, like other aspects of truth, are especially effective when they settle into the personal conscience prompting one to self-discipline and providing a firm standard for evaluating self, others, and society—and for discerning every human's desperate need for God's grace.

Most Americans, inside and outside the church, entertain a shallow view of sin—or none at all. In spite of the horrors of this century, these decent people evidence little awareness of the stubborn streak of insanity that runs through the history of the human species. They do not appreciate that something is dreadfully wrong with human nature.[1] They do not understand that the human mind is creative and pathological, compassionate and cruel, or that it produced, as Arthur Koestler observed four decades ago, "the splendor of our cathedrals . . . and the gargoyles that decorate them." Sin mars those who go to church and those who never darken her doors. It is one aspect of humankind that binds persons in self-concern, fractures relationships, stunts growth.

This book is written for people who want to get themselves together, to become authentic persons, to live responsibly, to care about persons, to be the kind of people who will declare under pressure, "I cannot and will not cut my conscience to fit this year's fashions."[2] It will be particularly helpful to parents, teachers, pastors, and public leaders. In the congregation, the book should be useful in teen-age catechetical classes, adult electives, church councils, and adult new members' classes.

12

Chapter 1 describes in broad strokes the current moral confusion that has resulted from modern man's failure to bring freedom and discipline into personal and social equilibrium. Chapters 2 through 5, oriented to the substantive claims of the Ten Commandments, outline divine-human relationships in personal context and human relationships in social context. Chapter 6 describes how one man brought freedom and discipline into personal and social equilibrium by fulfilling God's law, revealing fully the nature of God and man, and liberating humans to live in his redemptive community. The questions in the Appendix—listed chapter by chapter—are included to stimulate discussion, encourage critical thinking, and motivate responsible behavior.

My debt to Martin Luther's treatise "On the Liberty of the Christian Man" is evident throughout this study.[3] I am indebted also to two elemental Reformation traditions. First, to the Lutheran view of the three uses of the Law: to preserve the order of creation, to convince persons of their need for grace, and to provide a standard of obedience to God. Second, Word and Sacrament—the marks of the church set forward by Luther and shared by John Calvin and Huldreich Zwingli—are linked with Calvin's third mark of the church: disciplined response to the means of grace. This is the "cost of discipleship" set forward by Dietrich Bonhoeffer, the hinge upon which the church's theology must swing in our time.

Chapter I

On Freedom and Discipline

One of the most pressing problems of our time is that of bringing freedom and discipline into personal and social equilibrium. History demonstrates that freedom without discipline can end in personal chaos and social anarchy. Such was the case with the Weimar Republic, the decadent and self-deluding Germany of the post–World War I era. History also demonstrates that discipline without freedom can end in personal rigidity and political tyranny. The Nazi State, 1933–45, is tragic proof of the consequences of governmental tyranny overshadowing individual freedom.

It is also evident that radical shifts from freedom to discipline and back again weaken and can undermine the stability of a nation. The recurring crises in Britain and France since 1950 and in the United States since the 1960s should be viewed as red alerts. The failure to bring freedom and discipline into social equilibrium in the American Republic during the last several decades raises the question whether a liberal democracy can function effectively in a technological society set in a world community of competing and warring sovereign states ringed by scores of "national" unstable revolutionary governments. It would appear that without commonly accepted values (the working priorities that guide one's life in the world), it is impossible to establish a social balance between freedom and discipline.

Thus, the practical result has been that people in Western society opt for more and more freedom and accept less and less discipline (external and internal). The sociopolitical results of these flights from personal and social responsibility were predicted by social philosophers as different in temperament and outlook as Henry Adams, Oswald Spengler, and Walter Lippmann, 1890–1930. They are now evident to many of us. American novelist John Gardner, reviewing Walker Percy's novel *Lancelot*, observes how the hero, brooding over his wife's unfaithfulness, employs a "sophisticated modern sense that perhaps there are no evil acts, no good acts either, only acts of sickness, on one hand, and acts flowing from unrecognized self-interest on the other" and turns "his wife's sexual betrayal into a central philosophical mystery."[1] That moral confusion makes both good and evil illusionary. So Lancelot Lawar, in Percy's novel, sets out to be a monster. Toying with evil and lamenting the loss of the old values, he finally rages, "I will not have my son or daughter grow up in such a world."[2]

Our spiritual wells are running low. Our hope is waning. Innovation is being replaced by prefabricated thought. Creativity is being engulfed by mechanical methodology. Writing on the eve of America's Bicentennial, Sydney Ahlstrom, Yale's distinguished professor of church history, judged that we had come to "a time of calamities. . . . The American people . . . could see few living signs of the self-confidence and optimism that had marked the centennial observances of 1876, and even less of the revolutionary generation's bold assurance. . . . The nation's organic connections with the sources of its idealism and hope were withered."[3] Tested values that once seemed right and that were unassailable in some quarters of society have been badly shaken.

On Freedom and Discipline

Since the Renaissance, the values of Western society have been under stress and attack. Both were accelerated by the Industrial Revolution of the eighteenth century and shoved into high gear by the impact of two world wars. The shattering came during the unprecedented technological revolution beginning with World War II. Centuries-old values have been wiped out, leaving only lip service behind. Thomas Luckman compares our citizens' evolution of moral options with the way they shop for food brands—according to personal taste, social position, and economic resources. Their privatized values provide neither base nor direction for persons to mature or to fashion a stable, just society.[4]

The axial points in our lives are ground to the core. Personal vulnerability is at the center of our social, economic, and political existence. The collapse of moral constancy is evident everywhere. American historian Andrew Hacker concludes that we are no longer a nation of people but a collection of two hundred million egos, each pursuing its own narrow purposes. We must come to terms first with ourselves and then with our fellow humans. That means that we, who are creatures, must come to terms first with God, who is the creator, if this nation is to endure as a "government of the people, by the people, and for the people."

In Western society, and in the United States in particular, the central problem is the crisis in moral responsibility among the citizenry. Alistair Cooke, commenting on his American television series "America" several years ago opined:

I myself think I recognize here several of the symptoms that Edward Gibbon maintained were signs of the decline of Rome. . . . A mounting love of show and luxury. A widening gap between the very rich and the very poor. An obsession with sex. Freakishness in the arts masquerading as originality. . . . In the past decade America has demonstrated the Roman folly of exercising military might in places remote from the centers of power. . . . In this country—a land of the most persistent idealism and the blandest cynicism—the race is on between its decadence and its vitality.[5]

17

But there is a radical difference between the Roman era and the American era. In the first three centuries A.D., the church—a revolutionary community of faith—offered new life through submission to the person and ethic of Jesus. It also provided the only bridge from Roman times through the Dark Ages to medieval culture. Today, the church in most sectors of Western society is part of the problem. Its preoccupation with institutional survival exhausts its already thin energies and shallow resources. Where, then, can we turn?

Like Luther and Calvin, Barth and Niebuhr, we can go to God's Word. Archbishop of Canterbury Donald Coggan suggested a solid place to begin as he commented on the moral chaos in the West in the mid-1970s: "There's a lot to be said for the Ten Commandments." Coggan's observation takes on immediate and far-reaching significance when the substance of the Commandments is evaluated against the collapse of moral constancy in our era. Another respected churchman, an American preacher, Harry Emerson Fosdick, then in retirement, put it strongly two decades before Coggan became archbishop.

In my callow youth I reached the conclusion that we had so far spiritually progressed that we could center all attention on Paul's positive ethic, "Love is the fulfilling of the law," and that we need no longer stress the negative "Thou shalt not." I take it back. I know human life better. I wish those Ten Commandments could be blazoned in every market place, in every schoolhouse, in every church.

> Thou shalt not kill.
> Thou shalt not commit adultery.
> Thou shalt not steal.
> Thou shalt not bear false witness.
> Thou shalt not covet.[6]

Professor Kai Erikson of Yale University observed late in 1976 that "a world without stable points of reference is a world in ruins for those who find themselves without the personal resources or the good luck to navigate effectively in it."[7] The Ten Commandments, taken as elemental guides, provide those stable points. Handled realistically, they point up the boundaries of the freedom we prize. Understood biblically, they provide the guides that correct and challenge us to use freedom responsibly by coming under God's authority.

The fact that the second tablet of the Commandments (four through ten: respect for parents, human life, property, marriage, truth, human personality) can provide a moral base outside a strictly Christian context must not blind Protestant, Catholic, and Orthodox church members to their own urgent need to recover the Law as a positive force in their practice of the Christian life. Their lives, except for a minority, are not more disciplined or their values more durable than those of their neighbors outside the church. Their present reliance on cheap grace or social deeds or ritual has not transformed them into seriously concerned citizens who work corporately for social justice or into persons who care intensely about other persons beyond their own family, class, nation, or race. The church's disregard for the Commandments, especially in the decades after World War I, is part of the current social problem.

God's Word includes law and gospel, demand and promise. Either apart from the other distorts his Word. Paul urged the early church to teach and live by both, which, taken together, he identified as "the whole counsel of God." The Reformers, particularly Luther, divided the Word into law and gospel for teaching purposes, but neither he nor Paul separated them. The seventeenth-century English and the New England Puritans, viewing the Ten Commandments as "commands with promise," did not rely on cheap grace. Their theology was more than moralism. From an evangelical point of view, they were limited in their understanding of God's grace, but they had—as many contemporary evangelicals do not have—a sober respect for God's moral demands in social context. They

19

believed vigorously in one of historian Charles A. Beard's laws of history: "The mills of the gods grind slowly, but they grind exceeding fine." But most post-Reformation church members failed to keep law and gospel in balance (tension). Some concentrated on the demands of God; others focused on his grace. Because these one-sided emphases prevail today, especially in the congregations, the church is hamstrung in its efforts to act. The demands of God separated from his promises drive people to despair, turn them off, or produce legalism. The promises of God proclaimed apart from his commandments atrophy people's capacity for becoming responsible citizens and whole persons. The widespread lack of equilibrium between freedom and discipline in our personal and social-political lives poses a deep theological problem for the twentieth-century church and a philosophical and practical problem for every political society.

Herbert Butterfield, a British Christian historian, urges that we hold fast to Christ and loosely to all else. That is sound counsel if one resists the current heretical "Jesus religion," which sees salvation only in personal terms. To focus properly on the biblical Jesus—the Jesus of history—we are required to lay hold of both the law and the prophets as he did. Jesus did not ignore or destroy them. He gave new meaning to the former, enlarged the insights of the latter, and applied those insights trenchantly (sometimes divisively: he who is not *with* me is *against* me). He declared flatly that if we do not understand Moses we cannot understand him (John 5:46-47).

The whole church—mainline Protestantism, Catholicism, evangelicals, charismatics—needs to reclaim the Old Testament tradition in depth and then to learn how Jesus handled it. Demand and promise are inseparable in biblical religion. Too many men and women of the church, like humanists and politicians, make promises without underscoring their moral mandates. Promise without righteousness—like moralism, legalism, and human pietism—invalidates the biblical message. "One can only hear the judgment of the law when it is accompanied by the healing of the gospel, and one can only hear the gospel when it is accompanied by the law."[8] It is also true that the politics of promise separated from socioeconomic responsibility has strained public confidence in the government.[9] Political promises without demands breed disillusionment and despair. The need for equilibrium has never been greater.

Our moral dilemma, inside and outside the church, is acute. Millions of persons in our generation simply do not know—and many no longer care, intellectually or existentially—that there is a right and wrong or that one is different from the other. We have become too permissive with ourselves and therefore with others. Self-discipline leads to freedom in the context of social behavior: a rising sense of responsibility. Before the call to self-discipline makes sense, however, values must be identified honestly and defined clearly. One scale of values must be affirmed broadly to be right and the other rejected broadly as wrong. The Ten Commandments provide solid guidance here. Read in biblical-social context, they offer valid restraints, wholesome correctives, and firm measures for one's private and public self and for evaluating other selves objectively.

These broad measures are also crucial for maintaining a liberal (individual rights guaranteed by law) democracy. Otherwise, the state, arguing national interest abroad and social order at home, will assume control over its people's individual liberties. It is the function of morality to civilize broad conceptions of national interest abroad and to balance the citizen's view of individual rights in fashioning a stable society at home. The civil rights movement and the Vietnam debate in the 1960s, reflecting in both situations a moral stance, did influence America's domestic and national policies. This theory of the function of public morality is workable. Indeed, it is basic to liberal democracy as our founding fathers declared it to be. Its application depends on the moral principles, the operative value system of the nation's citizenry. The Ten Commandments are relevant socially and politically. Basic morality and representative government—as Franklin and Washington, Adams and Jefferson, perceived and taught—go hand in hand. The latter cannot exist long without the former. Presently, too many Americans have lost sight of that or no longer believe it.

Millions of Americans confess openly that their lives don't hold together as they once did, that fewer and fewer things seem to be certain.

Archie Bunker—is more than a robot who views the world in terms of good guys and bad guys. Archie is more than a hard-hat with a penchant for the past. In his ignorant and emotive way he evokes the recognition that something at the heart of things is giving out on us. And it is not just a consequence of the pressure for change; they have always been with us. There is an erosion at the core. . . . We are experiencing a shift in vulnerability from the periphery to the center.[10]

The Ten Commandments remind us of the universal axiom that there are times in each individual's growth in personhood when "no" is the only effective counsel. For our generation, this kind of negative injunction can be a positive directive. Church people too must recover the truth that they especially are called to be responsible citizens. Without just and humane sociopolitical structures it is difficult for all citizens and impossible for some to develop meaningful human relationships.

Since World War I, millions in the West, the majority of church members among them, have succumbed to one form or other of "positive thinking" and privatistic behavior, getting farther and farther away from the biblical view of human nature and corporate living. It was Émile Coué in the 1920s, Norman Vincent Peale in the 1950s, "piety on the Potomac" in the 1960s, and "possibility thinking" in the 1970s. The popular appeal of pop psychologies in each generation points up every human's strong bent against self-discipline and social responsibility. People yearn for meaning in their lives, but they want it without discipline and without serious social involvement.[11] This widening search among our citizenry for personal Shangri-las gives substance to Philip Slater's frightening description of the American people's selfish retreat into individualism.[12]

But history's ambiguities do not yield to paper-thin psychologies of hope. The harsh social-economic-political inequities in and among nations are not altered without responsible work in political structures by elected representatives and concerned citizens. Human sin is deep-seated, stubborn, mysterious. "The saints were not talking nonsense when they called themselves the greatest sinners. The goal of perfectability is a bastardized concept smuggled into ethics from technology, and results from a confusion between the two."[13] Human and social perfectibility are illusions. Disasters strike around us. Defections occur in us. We manipulate others, and we are manipulated. Our bureaucratic structures institutionalize on a large scale the evil in our persons. In this technological era, it is our flawed selves and other flawed selves that we fear, screened from personal responsibility by our bureaucracies.

Nuclear weapons—indeed all technological implements—are not moral, immoral, or amoral. Degrees of morality attach only to human beings. Nuclear scientists and military specialists warn that, in 1978, we have thirty minutes to retaliate if Russia rains missiles on us. Obviously, Russia also has thirty minutes to retaliate if we attack them. We fear them and they fear us, because instinctively, we and they fear ourselves. Nonetheless, both Russians and Americans eat, drink, try to be happy, and do business as usual. Human nature, flawed by sin, is not repaired by threats any more than by cheap assurances, cosmetic social reforms, or treaties.

Shallow psychoreligious formulas linked with a chauvinistic civil religion or an uncritical devotion to the Bible (biblicism) do not stir enthusiasms strong enough to equip us to live responsibly in today's unstable, violent world. Personal meditation based on a guru's secret word may lower one's blood pressure and produce a shallow sense of well-being, but it will not transform human nature or motivate ego-centered human beings to build a just society for the sake of the kingdom of God. Just as freedom and discipline still stand over against each other in human society, so freedom becomes anarchy and discipline becomes fascism in one corner of the world after another.

But words like *discipline* and *responsibility* are not fashionable these days; the word *authority* threatens people who are hung-up on doing their own thing, committed to life-styles that please them, and—lacking a sense of history—persuaded that they produce their own ideas from nothing. So, these persons are hoisted on their own petard. If persons are to be fulfilled and live purposefully in society and if social justice and social stability are to be actualized, individuals and their social institutions will have to come to terms with the realities of discipline and freedom, responsibility and authority. The Mosaic moral law, framed by God's grace, collided head-on with the Israelites' natural desires and self-serving deeds. It may sharpen our perception of our times to say boldly that just as the Ten Commandments had an undebatable relevance for Moses' people, so has its basic teaching an enduring significance and meaning for all times. They are new in our time because, as in Moses' day, most people do not have working priorities that guide their lives.

An unreasoned, unrestricted doing of what comes naturally in any generation leads to personal disorientation and social disorder. That is one reason why God had to rescue his children from self-destruction. His primary motivation, of course, was rooted in his indefatigable love. He made a covenant with Israel promising them his presence and power. In the Commandments he defined their part in honoring that covenant. He gave them his law as an evidence of his respect for human freedom, his demand for responsible social living, and his promise to help them grow into doing his will. Speaking through his prophets, God fleshed out his laws, and in Christ, he enfleshed his whole Word. The Ten Commandments, read in the light of Jesus' person and teaching, convict all humans of selfishness, point up human egocentricity, and encourage some to rely on God's grace. They are a schoolmaster that brings us to Christ. They provide direction and goals in the age-old human struggle to build humane communities rather than proud towers of technology. They reveal God who commands because he cares.

Presently, lawlessness, crass immorality, and unbridled egocentricity are center stage because so many hurt, damaged, traumatized people do not know that God cares. Their reckless ways of living invite the Four Horsemen of the Apocalypse to ride roughshod over the earth. The harbingers of their coming are at hand in America. Our cities are neither clean nor safe. The annual carnage on our highways is equal to our national war losses over a decade in Vietnam. The major producers and distributors of goods (automobiles, gasoline, gas, appliances, food, drugs, and much else) must be monitored steadily—and sued frequently in the courts—to protect individual consumers against defective products and unfair prices and to safeguard entire communities against pollution. Carelessness, absenteeism, and greed among the employees and the managers of our large industries have reached proportions that affect adversely the quality of the goods produced. Physical violence, widespread truancy, sloth, and cheating among students in high schools, colleges, and service academies, along with lackluster teaching at all educational levels, endanger our schools. Thousands of churches are fighting for institutional survival. Only here and there do any church institutions speak prophetically to society. Fewer show they really *care* about people by getting involved in their respective communities.

The American government too is morally insensitive. Having tried "war criminals" at Nürnberg in 1946, it shows only scattered signs of repentance for its own inhumanities in Southeast Asia, the CIA's attempts to disrupt foreign governments, the FBI's acts of espionage against American citizens, and widespread political corruption. The majority of citizens lack the moral sensitivity to demand that it do so. The breakdown in American family life since 1945 has become socially disruptive. By the mid-1960s America had become a "sexual wilderness" (see chap. 5). Many American homes were only bedrooms and lunch counters for commuters whose family members did not know one another as persons. One independent poll revealed that 70 percent of today's parents would *not* have children if they had it to do again.

Here are specific examples, selected at random, of this moral chaos.

John Gardner, executive director of Common Cause (a citizens' group of concerned persons), concluded in 1976 that most of the political process had become, in spite of some gains in reform effected by his citizens' group, "a vast game of barter and purchase involving campaign contributions, appointments to office, business favors, favorable legal decisions, and favorable locations of defense installations."[14]

Time magazine, late in 1976, reported a widespread evasion of laws that had been enacted to protect workers in the major industries.

Each year literally millions of U.S. workers are killed or crippled by job-related injury or disease. Six years ago, Congress created the Occupational Safety and Health Administration to solve this pressing industrial problem. But progress has been slow. . . . Last year 12,400 workers were killed in industrial accidents, not a significant improvement over the 13,700 who died in 1971. OSHA's first year another 2.1 million suffered disabling injuries. The Public Health Service in 1973 estimated that there were 390,000 new cases of occupational disease in the U. S. every year, and as many as 100,000 deaths; it believes that the figures are no better today.[15]

It is a matter of historical record that during the oil shortage of 1973 the top twenty-two oil companies increased their profits over 50 percent on the average. The fuel crisis (especially gas) in the harsh winter of 1977 is another case in point: the poor and the lower middle class bore the brunt of that national hardship. In the same year when the government, decrying the costs of public welfare, cut the volume of food stamps, Lockheed Corporation received billions in government subsidies of which millions went to Italian, Dutch, and Japanese government officials to guarantee contracts. In 1976, Representative Wayne Hayes was forced to resign, not because of his crass immoralities, but because his colleagues resented his high-handed use of power. Previously, Hayes' congressional district constituents had nominated him for another term because he had "served" them well.

But acting on the principle that the end justifies the means is not limited to corporation executives and highly placed persons in the federal and state governments. This Machiavellian principle is common among the American citizenry. Slum housing blights every city and crushes the spirit of millions of poverty-ridden residents because strict codes and tight laws are not enforced; the comfortable majority are unconcerned. Some families with incomes over one hundred thousand dollars pay less tax presently than other families with fifteen-thousand-dollar incomes. Welfare chiseling has reached epidemic proportions. From Amagansett to Aspen, from west Philadelphia to Watts, from Minneapolis to Miami, millions of Americans place convenience above conscience, choose comfort over character, and covet power rather than truth.

Four decades ago, Americans searched for their values in the Bible, the concerned neighborhood, the Declaration of

27

Independence and the Bill of Rights, Wilson's New Freedom and Roosevelt's New Deal. Today, American values are to be discerned in the national budget; the corporate reports of ITT, Exxon, Gulf, and General Motors; the socioeconomic plight of our cities; and the fierce poverty that dehumanizes a third of our nation.

Consider these two line items in the national budget for 1977.

The U. S. Budget, Fiscal Year, 1977, Office of the President

(Fiscal Year Billions)	1976	1977	$-Change	%-Change
National Defense	91.8	114.9	+23.0	+20%
Cities and States	90.2	63.4	−26.8	−30%

National defense went up 20 percent, benefitting big investors. Housing and other human needs went down 30 percent, disadvantaging further the middle class and savaging the poor.

Consider the increasing concentration of wealth in America. In an address at the Bicentennial Conference on Religious Liberty in Philadelphia in April, 1976, Temple University professor John C. Raines declared:

Today, the top one percent of the population holds 20 percent of all the personally owned wealth. The top two percent own 44 percent and top ten percent own 56 percent of all the wealth. The Land of Promise has become a land where 1.6 percent leaves an average estate of $185,000, while the remaining 98.6 percent leaves an average estate of $7,900. . . . Concentrated wealth translates easily into concentrated social power—power that can be used to pay for elections . . . and to purchase income tax and estate tax laws that benefit the few. [16]

Most politicians are reluctant to correct this economic imbalance through radical tax reform and other necessary legislation because too many of them are beholden to large givers. That is common knowledge. But there is a more potent reason: so many citizens, bucking for the next raise or looking for the next handout, provide a climate hospitable to the legislators' foot-dragging. Barbara Walters, leaving NBC for a five-year contract with ABC at one million dollars a year, said, *"It is the American way not to turn down a raise."* Anthony Hopkins, a 1976 Emmy Award winner, is reported to have altered his compulsive aggressive working style on television and movie sets because he had "reached such a state I was nearly driving myself and everyone else around me crazy."[17] Unfortunately, many other talented entertainers—James Dean, Marilyn Monroe, Janice Joplin, and Freddie Prinze among them—could not make those value judgments.

A quarter of a century ago, Budd Schulberg described this success syndrome in his best-selling novel *What Makes Sammy Run?* A half decade later, William Whyte's widely read study *The Organization Man* documented the organization man's surrender of personal identity for corporate security. Five years later, Sloan Wilson dramatized the ambitious, culturally one-dimensional company executive in *The Man in the Gray Flannel Suit.* Two decades later, in his poignant autobiographical work *What Shall We Wear to This Party?* Wilson declared—after a divorce, a second marriage, four children, genteel poverty, and a serious bout with alcoholism—that "the only real meaning I have found in life has been in my wife and children. Without them, I would be in more despair than a bankrupt millionaire."[18] But shaping one's personal values to the success syndrome did not happen suddenly after World War II. William Dean Howells, Theodore Dreiser, and Sinclair Lewis had discerned this American "cancer" decades before Schulberg, Whyte, and Miller had written a word. Horatio Alger's rags-to-riches books reflected as well as shaped the American success mentality after the American Civil War.[19]

The wealthy, the middle class, and the dispossessed—seeking the things one handles, tastes, touches, sees, and smells—created in turn the climate for Kennedy's politics of expectation, Johnson's politics of social engineering, and Nixon's politics of expediency. No society can survive long without its own working version of the Ten Commandments. Both the redeemed and the unredeemed need restraints and guides, as well as grace, to get in touch with themselves and others if they are to live responsibly in any political society.

God commands because he cares. His grace motivates and empowers us to take up our own burdens courageously and, at the same time, to shoulder the burdens of others compassionately. The Commandments are not rigid rules to be kept meticulously to earn God's approval. They never liberated anyone from sin. But they have kept many people from falling apart personally. It is the healing of the Cross that puts persons together and enables them to fashion true community. Even so, "new" creatures need guidelines too, especially in this era. To quote Kai Erikson again: "Human reactions to the age we are entering are likely to include a sense of cultural disorientation, a feeling of powerlessness, a dulled apathy, and a generalized fear about the condition of the universe."[20] It is to this human condition that God addresses himself.

The Commandments are the "new morality" in our era. They point up the structural weakness in humanity, underscore God's expectations for humans, and suggest a high human potential when persons claim God's grace and take his demands seriously. This triple thrust can help us today when pluralism, culture shock, and fragmenting values "have given rise to the modern individuality boom."[21] A nation of two hundred million egos cries out for inner guides and moral definitions of the boundaries of personal liberty.[22]

Voluntary self-discipline, taken up deliberately to humanize life—one's own and others' for Christ's sake—is Christian discipleship. A viable symbol of moral order and justice, as well as a specific articulation of that symbol in

30

judicial terms, is essential in every stable society. The Decalogue defines that moral order, provides the reason for doing social justice, and enables us to articulate it in judicial terms.

That raises the question of authority. We shall examine it in the next chapter.

CHAPTER II
ON AUTHORITY, FREEDOM, AND DISCIPLINE

> I am the Lord your God; set
> no other gods against me.
>
> Do not take God's name
> lightly.
>
> Do not neglect the corporate
> worship of God.

Americans are ambivalent toward authority. That is true, not only because they are human, but also because of their successful revolt against England, 1775–81, and their frontier experience, 1607–1890, which took them beyond the reach of the law. Richard Nixon's bald statement that the president of the United States is above the law is as American as apple pie. Most Americans—from the halls of Congress to the factories of Detroit—think they are above the law.[1] They are an undisciplined people.

In three centuries the American people conquered a wilderness, settled a continent, and fashioned their own cultural style in the context of "Western civilization." In that turbulent, violent, buoyant historical movement they proved that they love freedom and, under inner and external constraints, would provide a measure of freedom for others. During the first two-thirds of the twentieth century, coming-of-age Americans fought a war "to make the world safe for democracy," provided the muscle to stop the totalitarian onslaught of the Nazi and Japanese expansionists in the early 1940s, assumed leadership in establishing a world organization of nations, expended billions of dollars to rebuild Western Europe, and worked feverishly (bordering on paranoia) to contain Communism in the fifties and sixties.

But the effort to contain Communism ended in a humiliating political and spiritual defeat in Vietnam, galloping inflation, and deepening moral confusion. Americans, no longer able to impose their will on those they called "bad"—indeed, no longer able to divide the world neatly into good guys and bad guys—became confused in the early 1970s about their proper stance toward the world community of old and new nations, especially those in the Third and Fourth Worlds. Should these communities be policed, manipulated, fed, or accommodated? Should America retreat from its far-flung international involvements as it had after 1920? Trying first one way (confrontation) and then another (détente) and still another (covert intervention), and presently trying to juggle all three, the Americans proved their confusion.

Americans had demonstrated as early as 1670 that they love freedom, especially their own, and dislike discipline.[2] They questioned any authority that, in their judgment, limited their freedom unless they could see that it benefited them directly or indirectly. Two centuries later, even the "authority" of discriminatory social mores became questionable when blacks imposed economic boycotts. Americans—individualistic, idealistic, experimental, pragmatic, presently turning cynical—have always reacted immaturely (and often violently) to authority. Their revolutionary documents reflect their vigorous insistence on self-determination. Their frontier experience allowed them an unrestricted exercise of their natural bent for independence. Having pushed their nation from the Atlantic to the Pacific in a century of turbulent national existence, Americans discovered by 1900 that they had the material means to expand their geographic frontiers across both oceans. Their vast wealth, burgeoning technology, and belated entrance into two world wars, allowed them to exploit and victimize other peoples on three continents.

Three perceptive European historians—de Tocqueville, Bryce, and Brogan—assessing the American mind in 1830, 1880, and 1950, documented this American chauvinism. American historian Henry Steele Commager, appraising the American at mid-twentieth century, concluded his monumental study *The American Mind* with this unqualified judgment: "Two world wars had not induced in him either a sense of sin or that awareness of evil almost instinctive with most Old World peoples. . . . War had not taught him discipline or respect for authority."[3]

American church persons, despite their pious rhetoric, are also undisciplined. They are not disposed to accept authority—even the authority of God—when it delimits *their* personal liberty, challenges *their* prejudices, or invites *their* generous contributions of talent and money to further social justice. American church members have a shallow sense of sin, a limited awareness of evil as a pervading reality in life, and, like their unchurched fellow citizens, an unrealistic confidence in their technology. History demonstrates that all people want personal freedom, abhor self-discipline, and—when oppression gets unbearable—rebel against external restraints. The American tradition of individualism, anti-authoritarianism, and anti-intellectualism nurtures this human fault so that many now make it a virtue. When, for example, an ecumenical conclave calls the church to acknowledge that Christ is Lord, American church members respond affirmatively. But when these members are required to examine what Christ's lordship calls for in their persons, families, parishes, business practices, social mores, and politics, enthusiasm wanes, criticism rises, and contributions dwindle. Their fury mounts unless their parish and/or denominational leaders get Jesus back into "Bible times" and reaffirm that God sanctifies the status quo.[4] But until God's authority is recognized, acknowledged, and acted on, freedom is no more than a word to be savored, an idea to be explored, a concept to be fondled, a reality to be denied.

In their insightful *Religion and the Unconscious,* Ann and Barry Ulanov conclude that until persons acknowledge an authority they cannot know real freedom.

By directing allegiance to an extramundane authority, religion provides the individual person with a frame of reference that transcends the mass-mindedness of modern society. Such empirical awareness of an intensely personal reciprocal relationship between one's self and the otherness of this other-worldly authority protects the individual from submersion in the mass. It provides the basis of individual freedom and authority.[5]

All persons need the freedom that their acknowledgment of the authority of God can guarantee. The first three commandments offer a disciplined way to connect with that authority. Rooted in and reflecting "an extramundane authority," these commandments underscore God's sovereignty; they call people to obedience in freedom as their right relationship with God. "I am who I am," declares Yahweh. The very declaration of the word EGO stands for the personality and life of God. He stands as the subject; humanity stands as his object. The sovereign God of the scriptures declares, "I will not tolerate any second subject, any other God" (Isaiah 45:5, 23; 43:11; 44:6). The first three commandments define every human's proper exercise of freedom as the acceptance of God's sovereign authority and active trust in his parental love. God's commands come with promise; they are divine love in action.

In the first table of the Decalogue, God counsels us to

acknowledge his absolute sovereignty (no other gods to be set against him), to seal our relationship with him by integrity (honor his name by doing his commandments), and to worship him (assemble with his people to remember his goodness and to learn his purposes). Jesus did not destroy the counsel of his Father. He accepted and honored it. He also made it more encompassing. In Jesus' hands the first commandment reads: Seek first the kingdom of God and everything necessary for authentic life will be given to you. He enlarged the second to read: If you love me, do my commandments. He undergirded the third with the staggering promise that where two or three are gathered in his name, he would be present with them.

These divine commands for priority, integrity, and obedience in freedom reprove, correct, and challenge us to recognize and live under God's authority. They outline the narrow gate to which Jesus pointed centuries later as the only way into free and whole life. Law and gospel make up the whole counsel of God. As children need to be taught that fire hurts as well as helps, so adults need to learn that self-discipline shaped to God's authority is the only road to freedom. Just as teen-agers need specific guidelines for discerning the nature of responsible personhood, adults also require solid definitions of moral boundaries at all stages in their experience. When a substantial bloc of a nation's citizens do what is right in their sight without serious regard for the rights of others, the need for a vigorous clarification of values is crucial. Such is the American condition.

I

The first commandment calls us to recognize reality: everyone and everything originates with the Lord God of life. Creation is his first act of grace, even as sustenance is his continuing act of grace, and redemption is his ultimate act of grace. Human beings, animals and birds and fish, the earth, and the incomprehensible universe depend on God's creative, sustaining, and renewing power. Quantum physics theorizes on this view of creation and re-creation; environmentalism demonstrates it; Genesis proclaims it; Jesus embodies it.

In a day of organ transplants, genetic engineering, space exploration, exploitation of natural resources, and the threat of nuclear destruction, the first commandment calls us from illusion to reality. Our heady scientific climate, fed by a galloping technology and an unparalleled affluence, tempts us to ignore the true source and sustainer of life. We think of ourselves as the creators and sustainers. Modern people, astride their pyramiding technology, are uncomfortable with their creaturehood. Culturally conditioned by scientism and insulated by affluence, Western people, especially in America, behave as though they had fashioned themselves, their mates, their children, and their world. So Barbara Tuchman's *Proud Tower*, in which she describes the excesses of nationalistic egoism that unleashed World War I, reminds one of the Bible's Tower of Babel![6] When these breakdowns in basic social responsibility are understood theologically, we come face to face with corporate idolatry. We have fallen under the sway of false gods and made ourselves and our institutions to be gods. We have denied our creaturehood. Our proud tower has fallen. Our confidence in ourselves is badly shaken. The recognition and acceptance of our creaturehood make the sane exercise of human freedom possible.

In this era of illusion and empty rhetoric, the first commandment calls us to face the limitations of our creaturehood. We are neither gods nor demigods. We are bold discoverers and ingenious inventors, but we are not creators. We possess nothing that we have not been given. God alone has the ability to imagine and create the forms and beings revealed magnificently in the planet earth and the cosmos, the panther and the redwood, the newborn infant and the mysterious healing powers of the human body. But our preoccupation with our proud towers has blinded us to the magnificent truth that God has fashioned human beings to embody his likeness. The first commandment can help us to recover the insight that, by his choice, he fashioned us for freedom and as his vice-regents. And therein resides the grandeur and the misery in being human. We can think God's thoughts after him; we can have the mind of Christ in us. But we cannot think God's thoughts for him, nor can we determine Christ's mind. The image (human beings) is not the reality (God). The image exists only because it reflects the reality. This is the essential meaning of the creation account in Genesis: all life is dependent on God.

The first commandment entreats us to remember that we are made for fellowship with God, to live in conscious dependence on him, do his commandments, claim his grace, and worship him in the beauty of holiness. Human beings exercise freedom most responsibily when they recognize that the source, sustenance, and redemption of their persons is the God who spoke partially through the law and the prophets and fully in Jesus of Nazareth without destroying either the law or the prophets. It is the nature of human beings, left to themselves, to turn liberty into license or self-discipline into drudgery. Like the prodigal, each person is free to seize life and squander it on himself or to come home and live under the Father's gracious authority. Like the prodigal's brother, each is free to live dutifully but drearily inside the Father's home, refusing his love. Each has the freedom to choose his lifestyle.

The first commandment also reveals that the Father actively seeks us out. He is not a moral dictator. He is not the Deists' clockmaker god. He is not Carlyle's spectator god. Yahweh is a loving Father whose concern for his children motivated him to reveal himself in his law, prophets and Son. The first three commandments, read in the perspective of the Cross, reveal the God who seeks us through his own pain as well as our travail. At awesome cost to himself, the God of Abraham and Moses, of Hosea and Paul, provides the opportunity for everyone to come home again. The dynamic for this new relationship is grace. Our Liberator's acceptance is given, not earned. Salvation is his work, not ours. But to accept his gift one must accept the Father's authority, strive to do his commandments faithfully, learn obedience in freedom.

A parable: one of Harvard's supreme gifts to its students three generations ago was George Lyman Kittredge, the Shakespearian scholar. His erudition, insight, felicitous language, and personal grace as a lecturer placed him among America's truly great college teachers during and after World War I. His person and his message were gifts to his students. But each student, to receive those splendid gifts, had to exercise personal discipline. Each had to elect Kittredge's courses rather than other courses. Each had to discipline his mind (critical listening, solid questions, careful study, critical examination of his insights) to receive Kittredge's gifts. So, too, must all humans respond in disciplined ways to experience God's grace.

Centuries after Moses, Yahweh, revealing himself in Jesus, invited burdened, broken, defeated persons to come to him for understanding, forgiveness, and renewal. At the same time, he admonished his followers to take up their cross daily and follow him. Underlying the unequivocal demand in the first commandment is the best of news: the sovereign God is not only accessible but does, in fact, seek us out. Jesus wrote that truth into history with his life's blood. But a vital relationship with him and a steady pilgrimage in his company require disciplined responses and bold deeds on our part. There is no computerized track into the kingdom of God. The abundant life that God offers is more than fleeting human satisfactions;

it is a gift of peace (being at one with God) that outruns human understanding. Peter and Paul martyred, Luther harassed and hunted, Wesley worried and wearied, Bonhoeffer and King threatened and murdered—all lived life abundantly. William Penn put it succinctly: "No Cross, no Crown." Jesus said, "Let a man deny himself daily." Self-discipline is the narrow gate that leads to whole life in real community.

The first commandment reveals a Creator who cares. It also alerts us to the human disposition to trust false gods, to test first one god and then another, and to juggle the demands of several gods at the same time. Moses' people worshiped the golden calf, were taken in later by the gods of the Amorites, shied away from the true God time and again, and centuries later, cut down his Son in cold blood. And *all* peoples over the centuries have repeated those deeds. The first commandment reveals the true God who recognizes this human weakness, alerts people to it, and shows them the way out: "Set no other gods against me" (Deuteronomy 5:7). To have another god is, in effect, to set that god against the Giver of all good gifts.

Modern men and women like our forebears, are polytheistic. Our split loyalties fragment our persons, divide our homes, polarize our communities, sectionalize our nation, and split our world into four unequal "worlds." Jesus declared that no one can serve two masters. One strand in the Hebrew religion is its insistent call to monotheism in a world of polytheism: there is one true God, and he is Yahweh. The genius of the Christian religion is that it incorporates the full revelation of this One who creates, cares, and elects to come into the world in the person of Jesus of Nazareth to liberate people and to make them whole.

Human beings are toolmakers, inventors of words, forgers of concepts, lovers and haters of self and other persons. But above all, they are searchers after meaning in human experience. They will, therefore, worship some god, whether it be mate, child, family, sex, money, power, or God, the Father of our Lord, Jesus Christ. Human beings are incurably religious; it is in their genes. As Augustine said: "Thou hast made us for Thyself, and our hearts are restless until they find their rest in Thee." The only issue to be decided is which god(s) one worships, which values one lives by, which life-style one forges. That makes human freedom "dreadful" as Sören Kierkegaard observed a century and a half ago!

Americans are too sophisticated to worship the gods of nature under their ancient names. Nonetheless, they crowd the seashore and lakes in summer and fly "the friendly skies" to the islands in winter because they are sun worshipers! A suntan is more desired in some circles than moral sensitivity. Other Americans worship the stars. Astrology is big business among the enlightened and the unenlightened in this era of scientism.[7]

Human creatures also worship other human creatures. There is the "my son, the doctor; my daughter, the lawyer" brand of idolatry. Millions of American parents worship at the altar of their offspring. They place their children ahead of God, if not always in their affections, certainly in their personal ambitions for them. Not many American families attempt to teach their children that the God of the universe is the Lord; fewer families demonstrate that they know or believe that he is. Instead, they turn their children into little gods and set them against the true God.

Another evidence of this human disposition to view loved ones as gods is common among many young people in love. The partners look on each other as "my life." God help them when they do, for in time, they will smother each other, turn on each other, or become neurotic together. One young man, breaking out of a possessive relationship with a young woman who adored him, said perceptively, "She was omnipresent." No human being is big enough or strong enough or wise enough or good enough to be another's god. Luther declared that whatever one sets his heart on and pursues is his

41

god. That god must be big enough to handle all one's needs. The issue then is one of priority. God will not tolerate second billing. He is a jealous God for our sake: No mortal, he says, can serve two masters.

Americans also worship false gods other than mates and children, the marketplace, the sun, the stars, and technology. They single out people in the worlds of entertainment, sports, and politics and make them their gods. To worship Robert Redford or Faye Dunaway, Roger Staubach or Chris Everett, is to impoverish one's own person and inflate the star's ego. But to worship a political leader is to damage the body politic as well as to mislead the politician and to diminish one's own psyche.

From 1933 to 1974, millions of Americans in turn placed Franklin Roosevelt, Harry Truman, Dwight Eisenhower, John Kennedy, Lyndon Johnson, and Richard Nixon above the King of kings. An ever-widening circle of citizens viewed the president as a superman, a being beyond criticism, a leader to be followed blindly, a savior set apart by Augustinian divinity. Forgetting their forebears' rugged criticisms of Washington, Lincoln, Wilson, and Hoover, they "caesarized" their presidents after 1932. Confused and frightened by a debilitating depression, total war, and a technological-nuclear-revolutionary world, the American people were conditioned culturally to trust power more than character, specialized competence more than hard-won wisdom.[8] The problem was, in part, situational. English scientist and novelist C. P. Snow observed after World War II that "one of the most bizarre features of any advanced industrial society in our time is that *the cardinal choices have to be made by a handful of men, in secret,* and, in legal form by men who cannot have a first-hand knowledge of what those choices depend upon or what their results may be."[9] The Manhattan Project, with its secret antecedents and, after the first atomic bombs were dropped on Japan, its secret enlargement and the advent of cold war strategies and subsequent missile diplomacy are frightening examples of this cultural reality. President Eisenhower warned against the institutionalization of competent specialists—he called it "the military-industrial complex,"—at the close of his second term. His warning fell on deaf ears. John Kennedy's New Frontiersmen were specialists recruited from the universities, the foundations, the science centers, the top echelons of the military, and the world of finance. How did such "rational," "cool," "precise minds" and "prim intellects" as Kennedy's, Sorenson's, McNamara's, Rusk's, and Bundy's—an administration of "all the talents"—take the United States "waist deep into the big muddy" of Indochina?[10]

In spite of the revelations on Watergate, the CIA, the FBI, the unprincipled efforts of large corporations to corrupt representative government, and lobbying by the Pentagon, a substantial segment of the citizenry still faces a large task in demythologizing the American presidency. Like the ancient Romans, contemporary Americans turned over their right to govern to a self-styled elite and endowed them with superhuman powers. The nation's founders entertained a more realistic appraisal of human nature. Like Lord Acton, a century later, they recognized that "power corrupts, and absolute power corrupts absolutely." But modern technology and the population explosion, as much as human nature, have warped the possibilities of and expectations for democratic governments. The first commandment helps us to face reality, get our bearings, and contemplate our need to accept the authority of God.

Mammon, Jesus' name for the god of materialism, is yet another powerful idol who commands the loyalty of millions in all strata of American society. Materialism reigns everywhere. As Jesus saw the problem, "possessions have the character of an idol. They can become an object of one's faith. . . . It is, therefore, part of the fulfillment of the first

commandment that we completely free ourselves of all bondage to our possessions. Under certain circumstances, Jesus
may demand that we completely abandon them."[11] That demand was placed on the rich young ruler. The youth, although
strongly attracted to Jesus, gave in to the appeal of his possessions; he chose mammon above Christ. Americans understand his decision. Many approve and emulate it; others
never make a conscious decision at all. One fears that the rich
young ruler would be approved in our service clubs, cham-
bers of commerce, and church boards for his common sense
and "realism." On the other hand, while Jesus commended
Zacchaeus for using a generous part of his wealth for others, he
did not counsel that tax-collector to divest himself of the substantial holdings he still possessed. Clearly, the basic issue here
is not money but priorities, mammon or Christ. Most moderns are in bondage, literally, to a material way of looking at life
because they worship mammon, the pagan god. This false god
promises undiscerning people pleasure, security, and power.

Money itself does not enhance or despoil the quality of life.
It is the compulsive pursuit of money and its evil uses that
maim the moral sense, sidetrack one in his quest for social
justice, and disrupt social order. Americans idolize money; it
is power. The attitude of American presidents to it is culturally conditioned. John Kennedy used money power to defeat
Hubert Humphrey in the West Virginia primary in 1960.
Lyndon Johnson amassed personal wealth on the strength of
his political power. Dwight Eisenhower, awed by money,
selected his golfing partners, political advisers, and Cabinet
members from the circle of American wealth. Richard Nixon
valued money more than his personal character and his constitutional responsibilities. Since World War II, it appears that
Harry Truman—"the lttle captain with the mighty heart" as
Dean Acheson called him—was the only president who did
not idolize money itself.[12]

In our culture, money *is* power. Worshiping it for its selfish benefits, however, atrophies the human desire and capacity to grow into authentic personhood. But we are caught in a cultural web of our own weaving. The United States—with 6 percent of the world's population—uses at least 30 percent (some studies support 40 percent) of the earth's resources. Sunday after Sunday, church people declare that God is Lord over all and talk about stewardship, yet they contribute little for hungry people, waste food and energy, and decline to get involved in the struggle for socioeconomic justice in their own communities. Few church members write to their elected representatives protesting the nation's use of food for diplomatic purposes or to criticize political violations of justice at home and abroad *unless they are touched personally*. [13] The truth is hard: most American church members worship the pagan gods of abundance and affluence and their benefits—comfort and pleasure. They, like the ancient Israelites, are polytheistic. The ancient commandment "Do not set other gods against me" is as relevant today as it was in Moses' day.

Polytheism is rampant in every generation because it represents every human's way of trying to become his own god, setting his own ego on a makeshift throne. To some degree, everyone projects and worships his own reflections of God. And each views them as his own and not as *reflections* of God. A suntan enhances one's physical appearance. A horoscope supports one's itch to be different. Children are viewed as one's claim on immortality. Money guarantees one's security. So moderns set the false gods of their own warped beings against the true God. Homer, glorying in the Greek Pantheon; Hilter, promising the thousand-year Reich; Kennedy, hinting at Camelot; Johnson, calling for the Great Society; and Nixon, boasting about the American moon-landing—these no less than the ancient Israelites worshiping the golden calf crowded out the true God. The first commandment gets at the heart of this human dilemma: "Come to terms with your warped nature; don't set other gods against me."

But if human beings try to replace God, they also seek to shape him to fit their own image. Archie Bunker, attractive bigot in the television series "All in the Family," is not a church attender but a self-confessed believer in God. The following dialogue between Archie and his black neighbor, George Jefferson, demonstrates his readiness to shape God in his own image.

Archie: You an atheist?
George: No, I believe in God.
Archie: That's nice. . . . Interestin', too! I mean how the black people went from worshippin' snakes and beads and wooden idols . . . all the way up to our God.
George: What do you mean, your God?
Archie: Well, he's the white man's God, ain't he?
George: That ain't necessarily so. What makes you think God isn't black?
Archie: Because God created man in his own image, and you'll note *I ain't black*. [14]

Not only Archie Bunker, but conservatives, liberals, Democrats, Republicans, blacks, young people, feminists, male chauvinists, ethnics—all human beings and human groups—tend to see God, when they look at him at all, as an enlarged projection of themselves or their group, class, nation, or race. This innate self-interest allowed the American nation to applaud Bruce Barton's 1926 presentation of Jesus as a Chamber of Commerce "man of the year" in his widely-read novel *The Man Nobody Knows*. This cancerous self-interest allowed the nation in 1965 to accept and support a chauvinistic war in Vietnam. The human ego set against the true God (personal sin and corporate sin) is the most pervasive, stubborn, destructive idolatry of all. It cost Germany its honor in the Nazi era. It has cost America much respect at home and abroad since 1950.

The first commandment is God's red alert against the deadly human sin of pride. Further, Jesus sharpened the first commandment to read: "Whoever wants to follow me, let him deny himself daily, take up his cross, and follow me." This means in plain speech: discipline the ego; crucify the ego; allow the ego to come under God's authority. God is Lord. Human beings—mortal, ignorant, wicked—follow false gods as naturally as they breathe. Except for God's gracious deeds in the Commandments, the prophets, and in Christ, humanity would be trapped for aeons in the proud towers men and nations build.

The relevance of the first commandment during the last four decades of the twentieth century is clearly discernible. If the German church (Protestant and Catholic) had taken the first commandment seriously, there would have been no "final solution" to the Jewish question, no devastated Europe from Coventry to Stalingrad. If the American church (Protestant and Catholic) had heeded this commandment, the shame of Vietnam would not now burden the American conscience and the American economy—to say nothing of the awesome cost to Indochina. Leslie Farber, after thirty-five years as a practicing psychotherapist, observes: "Out of disbelief we have impudently assumed that all of life is now subject to our own will. And the disasters that have come from willing what cannot be willed have not at all brought us to some modesty about our presumptions. . . . It was only a question of time before man, in his desperation, would locate divinity in drugs and on that artificial rock build his church."[15]

"I am the Lord your God; set no other gods against me." This commandment defines the elemental issues of life and death in any era. Our persons—and our civilization—are at stake.

II

"Do not treat my name lightly." Recalling that the word *name* in Hebrew means "person," we know that this commandment calls for integrity in our personal relationship with

God. It is not aimed essentially at profanity or crude speech, although both are culturally uncouth. Instead, it focuses firmly on the elemental need for honesty in the human-divine relationship. "Don't patronize me. Don't try to use me. Don't caricature me. Don't try to manipulate me. Don't treat me casually. Take me seriously as I am." This is the essential meaning of the second commandment. Centuries after Moses, Jesus turned this commandment into a decisive test of integrity in every disciple's relationship with him: "Why call me, Lord, Lord, and neglect my commandments?"

Enduring human relationships are built on integrity. The divine-human relationship rests on it too. From Genesis through Revelation, God's running criticism of mild commitment never slackens (Deuteronomy: "Don't take my name in vain"; Luke: "Why call me, Lord?"; Revelation: "Because you are neither hot nor cold."). Human beings are careless with God's name; it is their nature to be. They are careless with all precious things in life—another's love, the truth, time, the earth's resources. They do not pursue righteousness single-mindedly. To Christ they sign themselves, "Casually yours." God warns against joining our person with his unless we intend seriously to go his way. Jesus, underscoring that integrity in discipleship is essential, put it bluntly:

Whoever puts his hand to the plow but looks back is not fit for the kingdom of God

Whoever loves mother or father more than me is not worthy of me.

Straight is the gate, narrow is the way.

The contemporary church violates this commandment on all fronts—preaching, teaching, evangelism, stewardship, worship, and service. Consider one particular evidence of violation: church membership. Many members of mainline Protestant churches check in only occasionally to take Communion or make a piddling contribution of record to maintain their "membership." These decent people who call themselves Christians shatter the second commandment. Church members who spend Sunday mornings with a good newspaper, playing golf or tennis, or sleeping off a Saturday night party instead of coming under God's Word in judgment and grace in corporate worship lack integrity. Centuries ago, God declared that he abhorred Israel's burnt offerings, the noise of their solemn assemblies, their pretensions, their devotion to form rather than spirit (Amos 3:18). He still does. Then and now, God calls his people to act justly, love mercy, and walk loyally with him (Micah 6:8). He does not tolerate a casual use or an excessive "religious" use of his name. But the contemporary church allows it. In fact, it encourages both sins by identifying nonparticipants in the life and work of the church as "inactive members" and by getting itself preoccupied with liturgies that rely on and propagate excessive religious uses of his name.

God thinks, feels, wills, imagines, creates, relates, suffers, saves. Architect of the cosmos, sovereign of the universe, he chooses to relate intimately with human beings. That is the unfolding miracle in God's progressive self-revelation in human history. A liberating lover, he yearns to be loved in return. He wants to be treated with integrity: heard, talked to, accepted, respected, served. He wants us to acknowledge him as our Father. He is heartbroken when he is rejected, ignored, or treated casually, not only because these responses cut individuals off from his family, but also because they wound him. Who can forget Jesus, forsaken at the close of his ministry, asking his disciples: "Will you also go away?" Hosea's deepest insight into God's nature is to see him as the constant lover. Brooding over what Gomer had done to him, yet loving her still, the prophet realized how deeply Israel had wounded God by her unfaithfulness: "Yahweh loves Israel the way I loved Gomer; therefore, look what our nation's sin has done to him" (Hosea 6:19). God loves us, forgives us, wants our companionship, yearns for us to come home.

Listen again to Hosea's remembrance of God's love call:

> How can I give you up, O Ephraim!
> How can I hand you over, O Israel!
> How can I make you like Admah!
> How can I treat you like Zeboiim!
> My heart recoils within me,
>   my compassion grows warm and
>   tender.
> I will not execute my fierce anger,
>   I will not again destroy Ephraim;
> for I am God and not man,
>   the Holy One in your midst,
>   and I will not come to destroy.
>
> (Hosea 11:8-9)

God takes Israel's sin seriously, but he does not fall out of love with Israel, does not turn his back on her, does not weary of her. His love will not let us go even when we break his heart. His love is at the center of the Ten Commandments. They are not the rungs on a "righteousness ladder" that we climb to get to God. Because God cares, he commands. Because he loves passionately, he yearns to be loved in return for our sake and his own.

This dimension of personal love is at the core of Jesus' revelation. John 3:16—"the gospel in miniature" as Luther saw it—is the best brief summary: "God so loved . . . " Jesus, asked to name the greatest commandment, answered simply: "You shall love the Lord your God with all your heart and mind and soul and strength and your neighbor as yourself." Love—his and ours—fulfills the law because it binds us to him. And we *can* love him *because* he first loved us.

Jesus, seeking to make this truth plain to his contemporaries, used the Aramaic word *Abba* (literally, "Daddy") from the common language of children in Jewish families. Employing that household word, Jesus taught and demonstrated that the sovereign God who creates, sustains, ordains, and judges is the same God who loves, accepts, forgives, and reconciles as a mature earthly father does. [16] And the nameless writer of the book of Revelation—pointing to the cataclysmic end of the world, the universe, and human affairs—comforted his fellow exiles on Patmos by assuring them that the sovereign God, omnipotent ruler and cosmic judge, would deal with the faithful as gently as he did when he was on earth as Jesus of Nazareth and that the awesome God and the compassionate Christ are one and the same.

Jesus demonstrated this intimate relationship between God and his human creation. With amazing grace, he directed his followers to use the familial form in addressing God that he used: "Our Father." [17] The Lord's Prayer is the Christian family crying, *Abba;* it articulates gracefully and openly *the* Father-child relationship. The first three commandments are descriptions of this intimate divine-human relationship. Because God loves us, he shows us where we are set against him, and he encourages us to get right with him, self, and others. These commandments then are not the imperious demands of a haughty royalty. They are the firm yet gentle pleas of a Father who cares for his children.

Still, the Christian church speaks too casually of the fatherhood of God. It often robs God of his righteous character. The German poet-philosopher Heinrich Heine epitomizes this modern heresy. On his deathbed, he was urged to confess his sins and repent. He declined, saying, "It is God's business to forgive me." So we too may attempt to use God—even as we used our parents and in adult life often use mate, children, neighbors, and co-workers. But God will not be used. His love is structured with his righteousness. The prodigal's father loved his son even though the lad had degraded himself and was dishonoring his father in the far country. But the righteousness of the father and the character of his household required that the prodigal come home and live responsibly on those objective terms—or not come home at all.

Disciplined response to the Giver of life's good gifts is an evidence of one's integrity. It is also necessary; faith without works is sterile. That is also true in human relationships. Wives have said to their husbands on occasion as husbands have said to their wives: "If you love me, show me." Most parents have said plaintively to a disobedient teen-ager: "Show that you love us." Pretense, play-acting, and hypocrisy corrode and ruin human relationships. They also despoil the divine-human relationship. Jesus said, "If you love me, do my commandments." His biting criticism of the Pharisees focused on their preoccupation with religious forms. Because he cared for them as persons, he attacked their hypocrisy.

We yearn for honest relationships, even as God does. We too have been hurt, sometimes irreparably, by someone who promised, "I'm for you all the way," only to have him sell us down the river. We learn, as Shakespeare remarked in *Hamlet*, that "one may smile, and smile, and be a villain." The church, scarcely less than the world, is crowded with "villains," and we come to the uneasy awareness that we too are "villains." Christ loves sinners, seeks them out, offers them fresh beginnings; but hypocrites break his heart. They also anger him: "Woe unto you . . . hypocrites." Christ loves sinners, but persons who address him casually on Sunday only to go all out for themselves from Monday through Saturday tax his patience, stir his anger, hurt him deeply because they close him out. "Don't handle my name carelessly. Don't relate to me casually. Don't pretend you love me. Count the cost of discipleship before you cast your lot with me. Then hang in there, because I am with you to the end." When Jesus wept over Jerusalem he was weeping for those who were ignoring his gift of new life. He was also expressing the pain of rejection.

III

The third commandment calls us to obey God: "Remember the Sabbath Day." Unless we remember him deliberately on one day of the week, it is not likely that we shall remember him on the other days of the week. Those who commune with God on a ski slope, at the seaside, on a golf course, in family conversation, or with the *New York Times* on a Sunday morning are enjoying God's matchless grace (his gifts of life, companionship, natural beauty, ideas). But in those deeds, however sacred, these people are not deepening their love for or understanding of the Lord of Moses and Hosea and Paul. From the beginnings of Christianity, Jesus' followers have assembled regularly for worship as this ancient commandment required. They assembled on Sunday, rather than Saturday, because God raised Jesus from the dead on Sunday, the first day of the week. In the year A.D. 321, the Roman emperor Constantine—having legalized Christianity a decade before—established Sunday as the legal day for Christian worship.

The third commandment is sharply relevant to our success-oriented, competitive culture. On the first level, it advocates a cycle of labor *and* rest for human beings. That is common sense. If one works all the time, refuses to refresh oneself physically and spiritually, one goes stale or breaks down. Bone-tired in body and exhausted in spirit, many earnest people grow weary in well-doing. In the Genesis account, the Creator himself rested. The ancient Hebrews, accepting God as a creative and creating person, concluded that he needed regular seasons for rest and contemplation. Having fashioned the world and human beings in "six days" he rested on the "seventh day." This anthropomorphic view of God errs in defining *his* needs, but it defines *our* needs precisely. Modern medicine confirms the Genesis prescription: at least one day of rest in every seven is necessary for physical, mental, and spiritual well-being. The emphasis is on restoration rather than inactivity or frenzied activity.

We are caught up in an activistic whirl, shocked by change, bombarded by noise, depressed by social divisiveness, threatened by nuclear extinction, disheartened by our own defections. We desperately need regular respites from both work and play. We need seasons and places for private meditation. We need to renew the human spirit. Recently, a handful of medical doctors working on human stress argued that prayer and meditation have a wholesome effect on the human body.[18] Christians have always said that. They have also insisted that, while prayers can be learned, the act of prayer is instinctive. James Carroll points out that prayer is "not a special activity reserved to elites of any kind—clerical, charismatic, holy, or desperate. Prayer is the consequence in human beings of God's existence, of God's act of I AM."[19] Because God is the source of our physical and spiritual life, one's whole person is strengthened through prayer—through relating consciously to God. To decline to pray denies the physical body essential recuperative resources that are available nowhere else. Erratic prayer stunts the growth of the spirit. Abundant living requires daily prayer in the spirit of Christ.

The third commandment also reminds us that Christianity is corporate. There are no solitary Christians. Privatistic Christianity is cultural; it is not biblical. We can and do meet God everywhere: in our closet prayer room and "where cross the crowded ways of life." But *he* also meets us specifically and regularly in the fellowship of believers where his Word is shared through preaching, teaching, sacraments, counseling, and dialogue. Christianity calls individuals into this unique community. There the Spirit nurtures and equips them for service in the world.

Luther observed that the growing Christian receives God's Word eagerly in the Scriptures, preaching, teaching, and sacraments. Faith comes by hearing as well as by doing. Actually, one's disciplined hearing of God's Word is usually prior to one's doing God's will. Worship is crucial to faith and witness. We must open our hearts and set our minds to it.

On Authority, Freedom, and Discipline

In the hour of worship the great drama of salvation is reenacted with the worshipers as eager participants, loved and therefore loving, understood and therefore understanding, receiving and therefore giving. For preaching, teaching, and sacraments; healing, evangelizing, and committee meetings; Bible study, stewardship, and parish administration, are not only means whereby the Word confront persons, but equally they are the means of encouraging saved sinners to worship God. Who can comprehend the power of the healing impulse that is born anew in the hour of Christian worship—the impulse to lay at the cross one's frustrations and hurts, hostilities and fears, self-loathing and self-praising. In Christian worship, persons sick to death of their own failure, brokenhearted over the betrayals of those near and dear to them, or frightened and wounded by the newfound knowledge of a killing disease find the power to begin again, to go on, to see it through, until Christ's victory becomes their victory too.

The church at worship also lifts with tender, strong hands those occasional moments of poignant awareness in every human life—the birth of a child, the union of a man and a woman, the death of a beloved mate—and fixes them within the structure of eternity. The world rejoices in the birth of a child; the communion of saints introduces him into life eternal. Friends wish the newlyweds well; the church binds them to each other by asking that each first bind self to God. The world offers sympathy in the hour of sorrow; the church provides the comfort of the resurrection of the body and the abundant life forever. The courageous rally the nation in crises to sacrifice; the church equips the faithful to pull themselves together and keep the world from going to pieces.

So the worshipers come, conscious of the transcendent joy that is available only to Christ's assembled people as they feed on the Word in preaching and teaching and sacraments. Who can remain isolated as scores of voices unite in singing hymns of faith; as the liturgist leads in the confession of sin, announces God's forgiveness, and reads the appointed scripture; as the preacher allows the Word to confront the worshipers with God's judgment and healing; and as persons, having made their offering in glad response to God's grace, plead expectantly, "Create in me a clean heart," then pray for the church, the state, and the world? Christ himself is present, and his people's hearts overflow with joy, peace, hope. His people know that it is good to be under a judgment beyond their own and other's judgment, and they rejoice in the one love that will never let them go. Answering God with hymns, prayers, and offerings, they covet every opportunity to gather in the house of the Lord.

Creaturelike, people and pastors go out to sin again, and they know it; but cleansed and strengthened, they also go out to render priestly service to God and humanity. Because they worshiped the triune God, some witness to a friend who is indifferent to the claims of Christ, others treasure the regained strength and draw on it in some lonely hour of temptation, and still others stand unbending in a hard controversy for Christ's sake, uncaring that they are judged unjustly by others, their consciences captive to the Word of God. In Christian worship are born the resolves to give up some hurtful affection, the insights that lay bare one's terrible bondage to sin, the courage to launch into life again, the desire and decision to follow Christ in the world.

In spite of the frustrations and failures that keep cropping up around one and in one, worshiping men and women see God brooding over chaos, leading his people across new Jordans to dry land, wiping away all tears. In Christ crucified, worshipers claim God's inexhaustible grace; and in Christ resurrected, they accept God's mighty victory over sin and death as their own. In Christ's church, real "community" happens because those who know they are loved by Christ can love him in return and from his love do good to friend and foe alike. As they go out from penitent, expectant worship, they are empowered to be a "Christ" to their neighbors; they are motivated to practice stewardship and evangelism and to engage in social action for the sake of the kingdom of God. It becomes plain in the preaching of Christ crucified that what one does with one's wants, needs, abilities, and time matter here and now. Constrained by the love of Christ, his followers get into the forefront of secular battles to strip away the power of evil and lay all things at his feet in this world. They expect no Camelot here, but they do work for justice here and now, because they are laborers in God's kingdom.

So with angels and archangels and all the company of heaven, the Christian at worship lauds and magnifies God's holy name, remembering gladly his manifold gifts of grace in the past, reaching eagerly for his gifts that are new every morning, waiting confidently and working expectantly for that glorious day when every knee shall bow and every tongue confess that Christ is Lord. And—as the wind blows where it will—the Holy Spirit, brooding over the congregation at worship, enables all who will to repent, to believe, to trust, and to take Christ's ministry into the world, going with the light that penetrates darkness, the leaven that permeates society, the salt that preserves the new life.

The first three commandments point up the dynamic for a new morality for twentieth-century humans. In the next three chapters, we shall examine God's mandates for doing this new morality in the family, the community of neighbors, and the complex community of classes, nations, and races.

chapter III
where responsible
relationships begin

Honor your parents; respect your traditions.

Do not speak falsely to or about others.

Until recently the American Republic has expected the church and the public school to teach morality to its children.[1] Neither has been effective in the last several decades. But in every generation, it is the family that carries, or fails to carry, the burden of this awesome responsibility.

Sturdy human relationships are established and nurtured in the home—mate to mate, parent to child, and child to parent. For good or ill, in joy and sorrow, we never escape fully our parental home and neighborhood. Both are with us from the cradle to the grave, shaping our persons through reality and illusion. We may remember vividly or dimly the house we lived in, the foods we ate, the parties we attended, the good clothes we wore, the Christmases we celebrated—or the hovels we shivered in, the hunger that gnawed at us, the parties others attended, the threadbare clothes that made us shy or aggressive, the Christmases that were depressing. But consciously and unconsciously we are affected most deeply as persons by our experiences with our parents and our siblings, their relationships with one another and our immediate neighborhood.

Everyone is also shaped by persons outside the home— peers, teachers, the parents of our friends, pastors, scout leaders, athletic coaches, and hosts of others. But it is primarily in the home that we learn—if we ever learn at all—to love and accept love, to forgive and accept forgiveness, to make and accept adjustments in our wants and needs in the context of others' wants and needs. This learning-maturing process is affected by the family's material situation, but it need not be determined by it. It is the quality of the human relationships that affect most deeply—for good and ill—the learning-maturing process. Who we are and how we function as adults are finally shaped by and rooted in our relationships in childhood and youth. Several of the basics in wholesome human relationships are tradition, personal integrity, and the desire to seek, tell, and do the truth.

God's call to honor living traditions, develop personal integrity, and learn to discern and tell and do the truth are the central thrusts in commandments four and eight. "Honor your parents; respect your traditions." "Do not speak falsely to or about others." We are admonished to be honest, open, and forthright in our family and community relationships. Do not lie to or about another person. Do not shade the truth to or about another person. Both commandments call for an honest, constructive, open stance in human relationships in the home and in society.

Jesus, accepting those demands, enlarged them. He directed that our *yes* be *yes* and our *no* be *no* with family, friends, neighbors, and foes alike. He pushed both commandments to their exterior limits: "Love your enemies, do good to those who hate you; bless those who curse you, and pray for those who treat you insultingly." In this life we fall short of those demands, but we scale them down only at severe cost to our persons and the church's faithful witness. To do so reduces the tension between what we are and what we are called in Christ to be, between the society that is and what it can be under God. In turn, this increases our dependence on the self and aborts our reliance on God's grace. Thus, we fail to grow in Christian personhood.

Integrity is indispensable if person-to-person relationships are to be wholesome, dynamic, enduring. No man or woman can relate authentically to his or her mate in marriage and no parent or child can relate wholesomely to the other(s) until truth undergirds and structures the relationships. Whatever is false corrodes and then destroys the relationships. Healthy human existence depends on adequate food, proper clothing, and decent shelter. But the quality of human relationships, given the physical necessities, does not depend on the things one possesses. It depends on the spiritual dimensions of the relationships we forge with others and with God. The horizontal relationship (person to person) lacks resilience, and often breaks down under pressure, unless it is joined strongly with the vertical relationship (God to person). The satisfaction in a person's life is enlarged or diminished by the significance or the triviality of one's daily work; but one's personhood does not depend finally on his or her work. It depends on one's relationships with mate, children, associates, neighbors, fellow citizens, fellow worshipers, enemies—and with God. Everybody cares deeply for somebody, sometime, somewhere, or his person shrivels away, no matter how significant his work may be.

What then are some of the marks of personal integrity in the home and community?

I

"Honor your father and mother; respect your traditions." That is where personal integrity begins. First, we must consider the original intention of this commandment if we are to get the full impact of it. Originally, it was intended to encourage children and young people to keep the religion of their fathers. It called Israel's youth to honor their parents' covenant with God and to keep their nation's traditions. God reminded the Israelites that he had called them through Abraham to be his people; that he had, through Moses, liberated them from Egyptian bondage; that he would, under Joshua, lead them into a new land. "Keep the religion of your fathers—remember what I have done and what I have promised to do. Recall deliberately your traditions. Remember your Creator in the days of your youth." Essentially, that is what the fourth commandment meant originally.[2]

That meaning is especially relevant in today's rootless society. Contemporary Americans have little sense of history. Their alienation from their religious, political, and family (ethnic) traditions makes it crucial that they recover all three. The public response to Alex Haley's *Roots* in print and on television is a dramatic demonstration of this void. Gibson Winter has pointed out that "America has been nurtured by two faith communities—a community of natural right and a community of biblical faith, the faith community finding expression in Jewish, Protestant, and Catholic forms. The civil religion of rights and the confessional faiths—were ultimately grounded in trust in deity. . . . We now seem to be at a stage where the confessional heritage is a last hope for renewal and liberation; but this requires a retrieval of the religious heritage."[3] That heritage is deep-set in the American experience.

Will the American people, who solved so many baffling problems and resolved some harsh conflicts in the past, recover confidence in their traditions? Will they adapt their thinking and their social-political institutions to the radical socioeconomic changes in the world since 1960 without destroying individual liberties? Will they retrieve their heritage of affirmation and expectation? Tradition, after all, can transmit meaning. It is the context for renewal, wholesome adaptation, and growth toward the responsible use of freedom. Nothing starts from scratch. In a real sense, the seeds of the American Revolution were in the Magna Carta as well as in Locke and Montesquieu. One can also make a strong case for Plato's *Republic* as a source.

Everyone has a past. The person each of us is today was shaped partially by his or her forebears and their experiences. We did not create ourselves. We do not fashion ourselves wholly. No one is self-made. We cannot escape altogether what our parents, teachers, pastors, friends, and political leaders were to us, what they taught us, and what they did to and for us. Like Ulysses, we are part of all that we have met. We live in the present, but we have roots in the past.

Like persons, nations also have open and hidden histories. What our nation is today was formed at Bunker Hill and Gettysburg, in Korea and Vietnam. It was shaped by George Washington and Thomas Jefferson, Abraham Lincoln and Horace Greeley and Harriet Beecher Stowe, Franklin Roosevelt and Herbert Hoover and Frances Perkins. It was molded by Roger Williams, Anne Hutchison, Tom Paine, Betsy Ross, Abigail Adams, Andrew Jackson, Nat Turner, Susan B. Anthony, Eugene Debs, Woodrow Wilson, Eleanor Roosevelt, Martin Luther King, Elizabeth MacAllister, Jesse Jackson, and Betty Freidan. It was shaped by geography, natural resources, industrial development, cities, and ethnic groups.

Every American Christian congregation functions in this national tradition even as it functions in the context of twenty centuries of Christian history. Many people ignore or deny this reality, but none escape its consequences. The twentieth-century church was shaped by the apostles, Augustine, Luther, Wesley, and John XXIII; shaped by Nicea, Chalcedon, the Reformation, and Vatican II; shaped by

Arminius, Constantine, Charlemagne, John Huss, Henry VIII, Otto von Bismarck, Frederick Temple, and Dietrich Bonhoeffer—each reflecting his cultural era—and is being shaped further by the words and deeds of laity and clergy in this generation. The church is shaped by its own traditions (which have been affected in turn by earlier cultural traditions); it is also shaped by the culture in which it lives and works now.[4] We need to know both traditions, understand them, teach what is essential in them, and discard what is outmoded in them. No human being, no family, no nation, no race proceeds *de novo*. God speaks to us most plainly in and through biblical tradition—the inspired human record of his self-revelation—interpreted in the light of Christ's life and teaching. He also speaks through persons and events in secular history, one's own human experiences, and the physical and psychical needs of other persons.

Presently, we Americans are out of touch with our political and religious traditions. We have much to remember and repent of; we also have much to be thankful for. Our nation's founders gave us a republican form of government that still works, however ploddingly. Their judgment that no president could be wholly honest, no legislator altogether objective, no judge omniscient, was realistic. No human being in any position of power can be trusted fully. Our Constitution's built-in system of checks and balances has been ignored often, but it worked effectively in the spring and summer of 1974. The machinery devised by the architects of our Constitution worked. A free press informed and stirred the public, and the public's elected and appointed advocates acted—some vigorously, others under constraint, but they acted. The judicial system declared that the President must live under the law. The legislative branch, evaluating the evidence, began to frame the articles of impeachment. The President resigned. The system groaned, but it worked.

When the Constitutional Convention of 1787 had completed its deliberations, it is reported that a woman asked Benjamin Franklin: "What kind of government have you given us?" The Philadelphia sage replied, "A republic, madam, if you can keep it." A century later, Woodrow Wilson, a professor of political science at Johns Hopkins University at the time, wrote: "It is a difficult task to live the life of a free people." In the 1960s and 1970s, the American people learned how difficult it is! We allowed freedom and discipline to get out of balance so badly that individual freedoms were in jeopardy for a season.

In our confused society—which cannot or will not distinguish between right and wrong—no-fault morality is gaining ground. The conviction that everything is equally good and equally bad will undermine our social structures. B. F. Skinner has one way of correcting this drifting into chaos: brainwash the citizens. There is another. Because the Ten Commandments reflect God's valuation of humanity, because they express a fundamental concern for personal decency and integrity and for social and economic justice, and because they are true for every culture, they provide a working morality for this era. The old morality—against which the Ten Commandments were framed and which is now practiced in the Western world as the "new morality"—is undermining Western civilization. The fourth commandment—a clarion call to honor mother and father—points up this claim. It encourages us to remember our forebears who settled and peopled this continent, cleared its land, bridged its rivers, dredged its harbors, built its cities, established its colleges and universities and churches, and framed the philosophic context and constitutional guidelines for this government.

There is another strand in the fourth commandment. When it was first set down, the head of the household (husband-father) had the power of life and death over his children, guaranteed by law. A man's power over his wife was also absolute; she was his possession. Jesus called for a radical change in this hierarchical, tyrannical, ungodly family structure. He taught that marriage is a partnership of persons equal under God; that children, God's gifts, are persons to be valued and equipped to grow into authentic personhood; that the family, like the nation, prospers under his lordship. Paul caught part of Jesus' teaching on family life. Like Moses and Jesus, he advised children to honor their parents; he also admonished parents against provoking their children to anger. God does not give parents absolute dominion over their children, and children are warned against manipulating their parents. The familial relationship is a two-generation community that adopts self-disciplines voluntarily so that every one can enjoy a larger measure of freedom. Each individual, valuing the others as persons, becomes more human. Neither, however, idolizes the others; God is the one who is worshiped. The family relationship, given by God, matures under his sovereignty.

But can a child honor an irresponsible parent? Millions of children throughout the world are conceived without love, abused physically, treated meanly, ignored shamefully. Millions more are damaged psychically because they are overloved or underloved emotionally. *Portnoy's Complaint* and *Looking for Mr. Goodbar*—best-selling novels in the last several years—demonstrate the current popularity of exposing and lamenting this psychical damage, real and imagined. But the problem is not new. It is older than the David-Absalom tragedy. It occurs generation after generation. The late W. C. Fields, cinema comedian, fled an unhappy home when he was ten years of age to live an undisciplined life until the day he died. Millions of children carry deep psychic scars into adulthood. Hundreds of thousands live daily in danger to life and limb. In many cases, the state or relatives or social workers or teachers or pastors must intercede in behalf of abused children. How then, in these grim circumstances, does this commandment apply to them?[5]

Every human being has at least one reason for remembering his natural parents respectfully: they gave him or her life. Apart from biological parents one would not exist. Each human being is the product of a sexual union between a male and female human being whether in love, hate, rebellion, or apathy. No matter how irresponsible one's natural parents are, each human being has an elemental reason to remember his parents gratefully. One's *unique* person, with its peculiar strengths and weaknesses, would not exist if one's biological parents had not brought him or her into the world.

Most parents, however, do more than create new beings. They provide food, shelter, and clothing for their children. These essential services, which require personal sacrifice in millions of American homes, invite solid respect from the children. In addition to giving life to their children and providing food and shelter and clothing for them, millions of parents also supply their children with educational opportunities that match—and in America, often overmatch—their abilities or self-discipline. Unfortunately, many American children, having received both the necessities and advantages of life from the cradle to adult life, treat them as though they were their due. Preoccupied with their own selves, they do not appreciate what they have received. Others, like the prodigal, squander their inheritance.

There are deeper levels in responsible parenting. Many parents who give life, supply the necessities of human existence with grace, and willingly—often sacrificially—provide excellent educational and cultural advantages, also share their beliefs, values, hopes, and *persons* with their children. Having created beings, they work to help them to grow into responsible persons. I recall frequently how my father, steeped in the Quaker faith, admonished me in my youth: "Let your 'yea be yea, and your nay, nay.' Always speak the truth, son." My father, now a decade in our Father's house, still influences my style of ministry as I work to bring the whole counsel of God to bear concretely on the personal and social lives of persons.[6]

If this teaching-sharing-correcting-forgiving relationship between parents and children in which attitudes are taught and caught is to develop steadily, it is essential that both generations tell and do the truth in love. Outside the boundaries of truth, we cannot learn to love, forgive, or serve others. Apart from love, truth can be crushing; but love, separated from truth (which makes it substantively different from God's love) is destructive. Truth—discerned, spoken, and acted out in love—is the only enduring foundation on which wholesome human relationships are built.

II

"Do not speak falsely to or about anyone." The thrust of this commandment is like that of the fourth commandment except it reaches beyond the intimate family circle to God's family. It calls us to speak the truth in love about people, events, and ideas. The strongest adversary we wrestle with in relating to other people constructively is not temper or sloth or boastfulness; it is deceit, deviousness, dishonesty, lack of integrity, disregard for the truth. Alert to devious people, we identify them as being manipulative, slippery, crooked, liars, cutthroats. We avoid them when we can; we keep our guard up when we are around them. Jesus suffered more than his share of hardship from dishonest, devious, lying people. When his public ministry widened and grew among the common people, the scribes and the Pharisees sought deviously to cut him down.

Failure to deal with truth on any level of human experience creates trouble; it often breeds chaos. Adolf Hitler's calculated lies at Munich and Neville Chamberlain's indisposition to face truth—coupled with the Nazi's immoral quest for power and the Allies' equally immoral quest for their safety at the expense of Czechoslovakia—triggered World War II. That war was not inevitable before Munich.

This unwillingness to tell the truth in all strata of American society is undermining the institutions of our society. Marriage and family life suffer new casualties every day. Multinational conglomerates (in the United States, Japan, the Netherlands, Germany, Italy) vulgarize governments (their own and others') as readily as they exploit consumers. Public education in too many communities fails to teach young people human decencies, citizenship responsibilities, and the exercise of critical judgment. That is true in part because the trust level between student-teacher, administrator-teacher, and administrator-taxpayer is dangerously low. The church too—beating a retreat from social responsibility and propagating privatistic religion—fails in most American communities to proclaim and teach the biblical truth about God, humanity, and society.

Of course, no one tells the truth all the time. There are the little white lies we tell—small acts of grace, some call them. "How do you like my grandmother's recipe for broccoli?" your hostess asks. "Delicious," you reply enthusiastically, promising yourself never to eat the vegetable again! On large issues, sensitive people often blunt the jagged edges of truth with compassion. Truth, told harshly, can hurt a person irreparably. Medical doctors, perhaps more than others, face this quandary regularly. Some dying patients simply cannot handle the raw truth about their condition; others can. To know one from the other imposes a heavy burden. Evading that truth is one way to handle the burden.

False perceptions, irrational judgments, searing prejudices, cultural shallowness, and a deep-set mysterious bent in human nature against any truth that threatens us combine to screen the whole truth from any of us. Some people tell little of the truth at any time. Many are unable, and others are unwilling, to do so. Both character types are poor risks in marriage, undependable partners in business, and treacherous threats in friendships. They are irresponsible citizens, often troublesome, some taking up extremist positions in politics. Senator Joseph McCarthy was a prototype. All of us are devious on occasion, and although most of us are not inclined to tolerate deviousness in others, we are quick to excuse it in ourselves. The eighth commandment is a mirror into which each person should look daily. Unless integrity grounded in truth undergirds human relationships, they deteriorate, disintegrate, or go sour.

Consider next three interrelated areas in which truth-telling strengthens human relationships and deepens social stability: events, ideas, and persons. The administration of justice inside and outside the courts depends heavily on each citizen's willingness and disciplined ability to tell the truth about events. What one thinks or feels or imagines is not at issue but what one can testify to factually about an event. Did the accident happen as the plaintiff claimed? Was the business contract violated? Did the commander of the German submarine that torpedoed the *Lusitania* in 1915 have advance information provided by the British Admiralty? Did Winston Churchill know beforehand that the Nazis would bomb Coventry? Did President Truman know that Japan was searching for a way to surrender when he authorized the atom bomb drops on Hiroshima and Nagasaki? To discern and tell the truth is the cornerstone of justice and social order.

One of the tragic policies in this nation's two-century history was in the making when President Lyndon Johnson misrepresented the facts about the Tonkin Gulf incident. He turned that insignificant event into the pretext for sending five hundred and fifty thousand troops into Vietnam without a declaration of war by Congress. Johnson's false witness and the expanded Vietnam war are inseparable; two and one-half million people died because of Johnson's duplicity, Congress' complicity, Kennedy's and Eisenhower's and Truman's lack of candor about Indochina, and our insensitivity. A chauvinistic nation's uncritical acceptance of the lie (until the Tet offensive) delayed but could not stave off the bitter fruits this nation would reap supporting Johnson in waging America's undeclared war.[7] Truth-telling about events is crucial in forging solid human relationships, maintaining a responsible judicial system, getting representative government to work, and easing and stabilizing international relationships.

The second area where truth-telling is essential is in reporting other people's ideas, statements, and deeds. Martin Luther interprets this commandment to mean that one should not only avoid lying about one's neighbor, but one should in fact speak well of him. That seems, at first, to be unrealistic. Yet, if one digs deep enough, one can find something good to say about anyone. It is reported that Hitler was kind to animals and that Al Capone was good to his mother! Digging out and telling these truths about those two modern-day bandits puts their monstrous behavior into a realistic perspective: they were psychopathic.

Luther understood and appreciated the spirit of this commandment. But the hard-nosed reformer violated regularly its spirit and often smashed its literal meaning. Erasmus had good reason to charge that Luther did not practice what he preached. The theologian from Wittenberg often spoke harshly and unfairly about the scholar from the North. He also spoke and wrote unkindly—sometimes unfairly—about the pope, Münzer, Zwingli, Henry VIII, the German princes, the peasants, and his fellow clergy. But he did *not* reshape the commandment to fit his personal failures in keeping it. He came under God's judgment regularly and accepted his authority. The commandment provides an absolute guide and measuring rod.

Jesus also said some hard things about people. He called Herod a fox; the Pharisees, hypocrites; and Peter, "satan" (literally, an evil adversary). But Jesus told those truths in the best interests of Herod, the Pharisees, and Peter. Herod would come to a violent end if he persisted in his devious ways. The Pharisees would miss true religion if they insisted on their hypocrisy. Simon Peter would not become a mature disciple unless he learned to rely on God's grace rather than his own resources.

Third, this commandment encourages us to tell the truth about other *persons*, their declared intentions, their possible motives. Ordinarily, people in polite company do not tell crude lies about other people; they are too refined and circumspect for that! Instead, they damn others with faint praise. Jones, doing a solid job, is commended for it in our presence. We respond: "Of course, he's doing well; his situation is hospitable. How could he fail?" Yet we know for a fact that Jones is doing a tremendous job. Because we are envious, we undercut him by belittling his accomplishments. Another way we break the commandment with "social" impunity is by patronizing others: "Poor John doesn't have the facts; we should be patient with him."

It is crucial in our personal relationships and in the interests of social stability that we—and our neighbors—tell the truth in love about other persons. *The Book of Common Prayer* admonishes us against evil-speaking, lying, and slandering. Luther's catechism urges us to speak well of our neighbors and to put the best construction on all their behavior. Jesus directs us to pray for those who mistreat us. A Christian reading of the eighth commandment incorporates all three directives.

It is not easy to tell the truth about other people, even under the most hospitable circumstances. When the other person's accomplishments outdistance ours or when another's vocational situation is more promising than ours, it is especially difficult—sometimes agonizing—to tell the truth about that person. For almost half a century, it has been difficult for

Republicans to tell the truth about Franklin Roosevelt and, equally, for Democrats to tell the truth about Herbert Hoover. Professional historians are generally more objective than their fellow-citizens, yet their scholarly accounts of both presidents are also tainted by degrees of partisanship. It is more difficult, of course, to tell the truth about one's competitor, rival, enemy, or friend than about a president of the United States. That is true, in part, because few of us are able to discern, accept, and tell the truth about ourselves privately and in relationships with others. That is where all of us must begin if we intend to take this commandment seriously.

To discern, accept, and tell the truth about one's self is a large assignment larded with pain. Benjamin Franklin declared that three things are extremely hard: steel, a diamond, and to know one's self. Socrates taught that the unexamined life is not worth living. Paul called for self-examination in the presence of Christ. Luther, in the first of his Ninety-five Theses, insisted on daily repentance. Self-deception is part of the awesome price we pay for being finite and wicked. Either we exaggerate our abilities and accomplishments or we depreciate them. Few people are as intelligent, gracious, or courageous as they think themselves to be. And no one is as worthless as the depressed person thinks he is. We all need to work at discerning the truth about ourselves, keeping on guard against misrepresenting ourselves both to ourselves and to others. Marriages flounder for many reasons, but one common cause is that one partner or the other misrepresents himself. Tragically, that usually occurs when the offending person is afraid to reveal his true self for fear of losing the respect of his loved one.

Adults, like children, misrepresent themselves— deliberately by artful design and unwittingly through faulty self-knowledge. This lack of self-knowledge among teen-agers is a basic reason why counselors and responsible parents oppose teen-age marriages. Few young people know yet

who they are or what they want to be or what they can expect
of themselves under pressure. Their natural immaturity does
not provide solid ground for marriage. Decades of living do
not guarantee that one will know oneself, but the added years
provide an advantage if one disciplines oneself to learn both
theoretically and experientially.

If we link this commandment with the first three commandments, we can read into it the call to tell the truth about
God. Consciously and unconsciously all church members
misrepresent God in one degree or other. For example, conservative church members testify: "God is interested in
me—my growth, my spiritual life, my happiness." And he is!
The Cross defines the height and depth and breadth of his
concern for persons. But biblical Christianity is not privatistic. The conservative has not told the whole truth about God.
Liberal church members err too when in effect they say: "Stop
taking your spiritual pulse. God cares too for the poor, the
depressed; he doesn't care about the well-being of the comfortable." He cares for the poor and depressed, but he also
cares about the comfortable and well-to-do, many of whom,
sunk in meaninglessness, cry out for a deliverance they only
sense. Jesus was as concerned for the rich young ruler as he
was for the beggar Lazarus. The whole truth about God is that
not one sparrow falls to the ground without his knowledge;
every person's travail is his travail. But the justice we claim for
ourselves he expects us to work for among our fellow humans.
The truth about God is that he saves us to carry on his Son's
ministry in the world.

In our era a vigorous recovery of these two ancient commandments could spell the difference between order and disorder. This sweeping judgment is not hyperbole when we
read it in the context of our time: the nuclear capacities of five
to eight nations to destroy others and themselves, the population explosion, worldwide poverty, and hunger and starva-
tion in the Third and Fourth Worlds. Deceivers, manip-

ulators, hypocrites, and consummate liars cannot fashion a stable society, a sane society, or a humane society. Compassionate truth-telling is the foundation on which wholesome social, political, and economic institutions are built.

Let us summarize commandments four and eight. Children, respect your parents; remember your traditions. Parents, respect your children; honor their right to become whole persons. Citizens, respect your self, other selves, and God; remember your political and religious traditions. Do not present, overtly or covertly, false testimony about events, ideas, or persons. Speak the truth in love. Be kindly affectioned to your self and other selves. Pray for those who use you meanly. Tell the truth for God's sake, your own sake, the sake of humanity, and to safeguard and extend social order with justice.

If the traditional values of Western society are to be reaffirmed and more effective social structures fashioned, leaders and followers will need to act out commandments four and eight. This requires our personal willingness to respect God's authority (chap. 2). It also requires us to act in openness toward other persons, recognizing, accepting, and rejoicing that we are dependent on one another. Interdependence is the theme of the next chapter.

CHAPTER IV

FASHIONING A STABLE SOCIETY

Do not kill.
Do not steal.
Do not commit adultery.

All human beings need God's grace to be saved. They also need his grace to become responsible persons. Martin Luther taught that God's grace is "the experience of being delivered from our experience." Paul Tillich emphasized the same truth: we can accept ourselves because God accepts us. God's moral counsel is essential if, in our freedom, we are to recognize our need for and claim his grace. The law is the schoolmaster that brings us to Christ.

Commandments five, six, and seven encourage us to hope and work for a just society, enlarge the stability of our government, and humanize our society. These commandments call humans to live responsibly with one another. A stable society requires a workable government, an adequate national defense, a sound but flexible economy, and a legal system that dispenses justice to its citizens. But these in turn require a solid moral base. Apart from that moral base a stable society may not be a humane society. Franco's Spain, Mussolini's Italy, Mao's China, and Iran under the Shah are recent evidences of that. On the other hand, a government that seeks to be humane has the responsibility to be stable. Otherwise, it will go down like Allende's Chile, which gave signs of trying to be humane. A society in which men and women do violence to the bodies or spirits of their fellow citizens and to the citizens of other nations is neither just nor humane. "You shall not kill." A society is neither just nor humane if its constituents seize by force, stealth, or legal deceptions any property that belongs to another. "You shall not steal." A society is neither humane nor stable if its consituents do violence to the families of their fellow citizens. "You shall not commit adultery." The good society takes shape when persons are valued above property, property rights are respected, and sex is viewed as a splendid gift from God to be enjoyed in the humane context of commitment, trust, and responsibility.

I

"Do not kill." Because technological skills have multiplied incalculably in the twentieth century, four generations of "humans" in this century have killed and maimed more human beings in major and minor wars, in insurrections, and in technological accidents (auto, plane, industry) than were killed and maimed in *all* the preceding generations of recorded history. Estimates vary from nine hundred million to a billion and a half people killed outright in one way or another in this "century of progress." Perhaps three times that many were maimed physically. All have been scarred, if not maimed, spiritually. The statistics stagger the human imagination; the emotional and intellectual damage is imponderable. Americans—no less than other nationals in the "Christian West"—have lived apathetically or coldly (except for minority protests) with the body counts first in the Pacific, then in Korea, and recently in Vietnam and with unsafe automobiles, unsafe rail beds, overtaxed charter planes, and unsafe school buses. Everywhere, human life is cheap. Technology has overwhelmed our thin moral sense.

Fifty years ago the commandment "Thou shalt not kill" stirred the conscience of many people in Western society. Today the issue centers not on the value of human life but on national security and human expediency. Human life is not valued. Americans killed fifty-two thousand people at home with hand guns during 1966–72, while forty-four thousand of their fellow citizens (five hundred thousand people in all) were being killed in Vietnam during those same years. Drinking drivers murdered twenty-five thousand fellow citizens last year on our highways. A century ago, we had killed off most of the American Indians, confining the remnant to reservation ghettos. Beginning in 1619—scarcely more than a decade after the first permanent settlement—we enslaved, then abused and intimidated black Americans. We turned our western desperadoes into heroes. We killed and maimed our own in the bloodiest civil war in modern world history. We atom-bombed the Japanese. We napalmed the Vietnamese. We tolerate gang wars in our cities. We terrorize our older citizens. We have assassinated 10 percent of our presidents. We have used food as a weapon in our diplomacy since 1960. We lean toward triage thinking at home and abroad. Rap Brown is right: "Violence is as American as apple pie."

Our national experience, as well as our human nature, makes this commandment against killing hard for us to take. So we modify it subtly and boldly. We should not kill, we argue, except in the national interest or in self-defense or to rid society of dangerous criminals or for therapeutic reasons. So wars, police actions, guerrilla engagements, political sabotage, assassinations, capital punishment, and abortion on demand are widely accepted in this nation. National interest, national security, political ideology, and personal convenience are the grounds that justify and motivate the American killings. But God gives no quarter: "Do not kill anyone, anytime, anywhere, under any circumstances." We desperately need to recover respect for human life.

Once the Israelites had become established as a nation, they engaged regularly in warfare. Their civil law was gory: an eye for an eye, a tooth for a tooth, a limb for a limb, a life for a life. They behaved like their neighbors. But their religion called them under the judgment of God's moral law. The fifth commandment fits all people and nations. There has never been a period in recorded history when individuals, tribes, kingdoms, nation-states, and alliances of nations were not murderous when their interests (as they viewed them) were threatened. The veneer of civilization is so thin that it barely hides human nature's bent to fratricide. And that veneer cracks easily when a nation judges that its national interests (economic, political, geographic) have been threatened to the point that its leaders call for military action. Recent examples are the advent of World War II, the Communist victory in China, the Korean War, the tragedy of Vietnam, the tinderbox in South Africa. Military action or political-economic action is taken when a nation (strong enough to throw its weight around) judges that its national interests are served by annexing, controlling, or intervening in the affairs of another nation. Throughout the nineteenth and early twentieth centuries Western Europe, the United States, and Japan exploited the peoples of Africa, Asia, and Latin America.

But that sort of behavior is old hat! Cain was a murderer when life went against him. Like other decent people, he had matured in a responsible home; he related to his parents and brother, and they to him, in his early years. Yet in a moment of violent anger surging up from the subterranean passages of his nature, he killed his brother in cold blood. His deed is as contemporary as the killings of the Kansas family Truman Capote reported on in his book *In Cold Blood* and as contemporary as Gary Gilmore's killing of two young men and the state of Utah's killing of Gary Gilmore, 1976–77. The Gestapo (Nazi Germany), the IRA (Ireland), the CIA (America), and the KGB (Russia) did not and presently do not view human life as sacred—others' or their own. The guiding principle for each security agency is that the end justifies the means. All human beings need the fifth commandment to humble them, sensitize them, call them to repentance, and guide them.

"Do no violence, directly or indirectly, to or against anyone." That is God's uncompromising word to all people in all times in all places. He admonishes human beings that all life belongs to him; he created it. No human being is so valueless in God's sight that we dare to take it upon ourselves to isolate him in a concentration camp, dispose of him in a gas oven, eliminate him by capital punishment, or dehumanize him in war without coming under God's judgment. His command provides the absolute point of reference that human beings need. It allows no room for artful maneuvering: all killing is morally wrong. But would it be easier for us if God had made some exceptions to this commandment? Scarcely. If he had provided exceptions, we would have no solid frame of reference, no tribunal of judgment, no absolute guide.

This commandment requires that we inquire whether nuclear war can be a viable response to international tensions; whether nuclear control and then disarmament is in fact the first priority among the nuclear nations. The fifth commandment prods us to examine critically our economic imperialism. It presses us to discuss realistically whether national sovereignty can be tolerated any longer in a world of 130 sovereign nation-states. It also pushes us to face the deeper threats to the human spirit in modern diplomacy and war. What enduring good came out of World War II? What evils were thwarted? What psychic damage was done to the victors as to the victims? Churchill and his colleagues allowed Coventry to be destroyed rather than let the Nazis know that the British had broken their secret code. The consuming fire-raid on Dresden served no military purpose. Harry Truman insisted to the end of his days that he had made the right decision in atom-bombing Hiroshima and Nagasaki because—as he viewed it—he had saved two million American lives and kept Russia from getting firmly positioned in the Pacific War. A contemporary litany used in current Lutheran church groups studying evangelistic work, reads in part:

> Why did God create us?
> TO LOVE PEOPLE AND USE THINGS.
>
> How have we sinned?
> BY USING PEOPLE AND LOVING THINGS.[1]

Americans are a murderous people living among other murderous peoples in a fallen world. All nations—disposed to kill other people in their own national interests—need a commandment that declares categorically that killing is immoral, that all life belongs to God. From Cain to David, from Thermopylae to the Somme, from Dresden to Mai Lai, humans—alienated from God—have assaulted, maimed, and killed their own kind in real and imagined self-interest, in passion, and in envy. Human beings are violent by nature. If we bury God's absolute commandment against killing, we shall become lower than the animals that kill mainly to survive. And that, it appears, is happening.

American soldiers from the free world, educated to believe in the doctrine of inevitable progress and reared to view humanity as essentially good, walked through Dachau and Buchenwald in 1945. Shaken and sobered for a season, they were, twenty years later, running body counts in Vietnam, napalming the countryside to "secure" the area, and "destroying villages to save them."

> Three monkeys sat in a cocoanut tree,
> Discussing things as they're said to be.
> Said one to the other, "Now listen you two;

Fashioning a Stable Society

There's a certain rumor that can't be true
That man descends from our noble race!
The very idea's a disgrace.
No monk ever deserted his wife,
Starved her babies and ruined her life.
And you've never known the mother monk
To leave her babies with other to bunk.
And another thing you'll never see,
A monk build a fence around a cocoanut tree,
And let the cocoanuts go to waste
Forbidding all other monks a taste.
Here's another thing a monk won't do;
Go out at night and get in a stew,
Or use a gun or club or knife
To take another monkey's life.
Yes, man descends
The Ornery cuss—
But, brother, he didn't descend from us![2]

It is because we are not monkeys but humans that law is necessary, that self-discipline is sane, that God's grace is indispensable in building a humane society.

We cannot discuss here the many specific ways—other than war—in which modern people kill one another and themselves in a technological society: abortion, euthanasia, suicide, capital punishment, self-defense, drugs, overeating, drunken driving, and dangerous occupations (race-drivers, test pilots, riveters on skyscrapers, submariners, lab workers on infectious diseases, law-enforcement officers, etc.). These are some of the common ways. Some have become legally as well as morally complex: the Karen Quinlan case (euthanasia), the trial of Doctor Herbert Edelin of Boston (abortion), the execution of Gary Gilmore (capital punishment), and the CIA-planned assassinations. Moral judgments differ radically on these and other life issues. Ambiguous, they call for inter-disciplinary study (ethical, medical, legal, theological, social, political, economic). They will not be resolved easily.

But our primary purpose here is to underscore the *absolute* character of the fifth commandment in a relativistic culture. However we respond to the new moral problems posed by life and death in a technological society—and human responses will be varied—the fifth commandment is firm: human life is sacred—only God has the right to take away what he creates. What is happening in our era is that we are being forced to redefine the *meaning of life* biologically and theologically, socially and legally. That will be an immense task for scientists, theologians, lawyers, psychologists, philosophers—and the public—during the remainder of this century. The problems will become more complex and controversial before we get broad working approaches in a technological society where genetic engineering, psychosurgery as a political instrument, and behavior control are at hand.

The fifth commandment is devastating apart from God's grace. It is crushing when we read it in the context of Jesus' teaching: "Whoever is angry with his brother without cause has already committed murder." He lifted the focus of the commandment against killing human beings to the killing of their *spirits,* leaving dispirited, dehumanized people to roam the earth as biological zombies. Mainline Protestantism and Catholicism have done little with the fifth commandment in this century. The Quakers, the Brethren, and the Mennonites have taken it more seriously.

II

"Do not steal." Don't take anything that belongs to anybody else by force or stealth, flattery or bribery, chicanery or manipulation. W. C. Fields, master of the old shell game, was sheer delight on film. In real life, his type is neither humorous nor innocent. There are, of course, many bold and subtle ways in which nations and persons break the sixth commandment.

America, after its fabricated war with Spain, proceeded to intervene regularly in the internal affairs of other national states with no regard for their sovereignty or for human rights: "dollar diplomacy," restrictive tariffs, active subversion, and military interventions (Dominican Republic, Lebanon, Vietnam, Panama). The United States was incensed when, decades later, other nations—especially the oil-producing nations in the Middle East—employed the tactics they had learned from this nation's "dollar diplomacy." Nonetheless, church members—like their fellow citizens—supported uncritically or chauvinistically the use of economic and military coercion to guarantee that other nations do our bidding. The use of food for "diplomatic" purposes, openly declared since 1960, is a particularly vicious way to break this commandment, yet it seems right to many. This nation—in some areas scarcely less than Russia or China—demonstrates grimly "man's inhumanity to man."

From the turbulent decades of Robert La Follette to the confused years of George McGovern, a handful of political leaders have raised their voices against our government's endorsement of corporate theft supported by military might. Others among our citizenry have asked probing questions and taken bold public stands—educators, church members, social workers, law-enforcement people, clergy—but the majority of American citizens have approved outright or accepted uncritically our national and corporate policies of theft in Asia, Latin America, and Africa. The United States has stolen from other nations, directly and indirectly, since the Mexican War. And its grand theft from the American Indians, framed in a century and a half of violence and broken treaties, is a chapter so dark in its history that it is not read in our schools or churches today.

In 1974, Secretary of State Henry Kissinger, reacting to the energy crunch, intimated publicly that the United States, if it did not get the oil it needed from the Middle East, would take it by force. Other Americans said the same thing more baldly. The self-interest of nations weighs more heavily on national decisions than agreements, treaties, alliances, or the uneven quest for world peace. Belgian neutrality, guaranteed in 1839, was, the Germans declared in 1914, "a scrap of paper." Tribes, confederations, nation-states, and empires break the sixth commandment whenever it suits them; they seize new technological means to get their way at any cost to truth and human life.[3]

This commandment also prods us to examine and alter the debilitating economic realities that presently separate those who are comfortable from those who are poor. Not many church members, the clergy among them, understand or appreciate the ancient Hebrew prophets who chastised the well-to-do for oppressing the poor and needy. Middle-class Protestant churches and their clergy (recruited from their own kind) simply cannot understand them unless both are converted. The majority obviously are not. The Old Testament prophets were flesh and blood men who cared intensely that the poor and powerless were *hurting* badly. With little regard for personal approval or physical safety they spoke out concretely against the political-religious establishment's bureaucratized self-interest, which ground the poor into the dust. The eighth-century prophets pointed to the crushing socio-economic differences between the rich and the poor in their day. In face-to-face encounters with the power elite, they declared bluntly that these inequities rested on personal and corporate theft. Their bold protests against this crass immorality constitute a rugged ethical strand in the prophetic tradition.

The same stern demand runs through the teaching of Jesus. It also prevailed in the early church, although it was not applied concretely against the state, because the early church had no legal status. The early Christians were, in the eyes of Rome, outlaw bands until Constantine, early in the fourth century, legalized the faith. In spite of this vigorous prophetic tradition in the Old and New Testament documents, many mainline Protestants, evangelicals, and middle-class Catholics insist today that concrete social criticism is not compatible with the Word of God. Some members curtail their giving or leave the church if the preaching insists otherwise. But when the grass-roots church acquiesces, and it usually has, it mutes God's Word.[4]

From the beginning, God has been concerned about how those who control natural resources, goods, services, and money treat those who, possessing little or nothing, are powerless. This aspect of the commandment is particularly relevant in our era. God expects that possessions will be used for the well-being of persons and that persons will not be used to get or keep possessions or to maintain the institutional church.

Theft, crassly open or legally concealed, roots in the human disposition to idolize possessions. Jesus did not reject the historical-legal practice of owning property. He owned nothing himself, but he did not attack the concept of private property. He taught that the prosperous and the poor should use their possessions—much (Zacchaeus) or little (widow and her mite)—in the service of persons. He taught that responsible stewardship values persons above possessions. He called for voluntary sharing with the oppressed and the dispossessed. He insisted that it should be generous like that of Zacchaeus and open-ended like that of the good Samaritan. Concluding his story of the Samaritan who provided help on the Jericho Road, Jesus advised his hearers to emulate the Samaritan's deed. Paul, appreciating Jesus' humane interpretation of the seventh commandment, pleaded with his fellow Christians to give beyond their means, to bear one another's burdens, to be "Christs" to one another.

In Christian context, this commandment calls people to be concerned equally with the material and spiritual strands in human life. It is a stubborn heresy in the church to separate the two; together, they are our human experience. The commandment prods us to share voluntarily, generously, and in disciplined fashion with those in need. Responsible stewardship is the issue here; and biblical stewardship collides head on with secular attitudes in the American church.[5] Most church members give what is left over after they meet the costs of housing, clothing, taxes, education, and pleasure. That is not Christian. Everything belongs to God. We are custodians, overseers, stewards, trustees of God's holdings for a season. Jesus urges us to be *risk-taking* trustees (see the parable of the talents). But the contemporary church rarely says that in concrete terms; it is too busy raising survival budgets. This commandment calls for biblical stewardship. Love is the dynamic; compassion toward hard-pressed persons and justice for oppressed peoples are the results.[6]

Persons, corporations, labor unions, governments, and churches are admonished by God: "Do not steal." Members of congregations who are comparatively strong in *giving* are themselves not distinguishable from their unchurched middle-class neighbors in their life-styles. All middle-class and well-to-do Americans steal in multiple ways from their impoverished neighbors at home and abroad, and—through exploitation of natural resources—from themselves and their descendents.

Recall the biblical account of Dives and Lazarus, the classic story of "rich man, poor man." It is rarely preached on in our middle-class congregations these days. Dives enjoyed large material comforts in this life, but he declined to share his God-given affluence with dispossessed people like Lazarus, the beggar at his gate. In death, Dives lost forever his rightful place in God's company; Lazarus was given his long-denied place. In God's kingdom, justice is done. "Vengeance is mine, I will repay," says the Lord. Victor Hugo, rejoicing over

Napoleon's defeat at Waterloo, put it this way: "God got tired of Napoleon."

The law of oppression is inexorable; persistent oppression produces revolution. With rising force, the earth's dispossessed are pressing for their rightful share of the world's goods *now*. When people who have much do not share willingly with those who have little and refuse outright to administer the earth's fruits responsibly or do it grudgingly under threat, then, in due season, the oppressed rise up to take away the possessions of the comfortable by ballots (Britain), bullets (Russia), economic boycott (Arab states) or military blackmail (the United States). Middle-class Americans had a microcosmic preview of this in the burning and looting that erupted in many of our major cities during the late 1960s. Equalization will come in America and Western Europe in the next several decades, whether by ballots, force, or the breakdown of capitalism.[7] The Third and Fourth Worlds will not be put down or put off much longer.

III

Crucial to the development of the humane society are personal commitment and fidelity in marriage and creative responsibility in family living. "Do not commit adultery." Originally, this commandment outlawed sexual intercourse with a married or betrothed woman on penalty of death. The sentence was carried out by the state, not by the husband. The original intent of the commandment was (a) to protect the husband's property (his wife) and (b) to ensure that his wife's children were his own.[8]

Jesus gave this commandment a radically new interpretation: full status for the woman as a person. But in doing that, he did not invalidate the unequivocal injunction against adultery. Forgiving an adulteress, he admonished her to "go, and sin no more." Paul did not grasp the full import of Jesus' teaching about persons (especially female persons) and, reading the creation account too literally, dragged the Hebrew hierarchical structure of marriage into Christianity. But in defining *spiritual* equality between the sexes, he did point steadily to the *relational* character of marriage: As Christ loves the Church, let a man so love his wife.

This particular commandment is specific: "Do not pursue your neighbor's wife; do not seduce your neighbor's husband." The meaning is clear: marital infidelity is wrong; commitment, loyalty, and mutual understanding are right. Tragically, Augustine identified "original sin" with human *sex* and the church in the West followed him in this heresy.[9] Consequently, many of the correctives of an unbiblical, unhealthy view of sex since World War I have been necessary and salutary. But in the decade of the sixties, the pendulum swung so far from a repressed and generally neurotic view of sex (encouraged by some segments of the church) that adultery has come to be tolerated, accepted, defended, encouraged, and even prescribed for "therapeutic" reasons. Obsession with sex is a new neurosis in late twentieth-century America.

The current sexual revolution in America, which had been gathering force since World War I, made its most decisive impact during the 1960s. That decade will be remembered, as Sydney Ahlstrom judges it, as the time of the "great moral revolution." It is his researched argument that this broad description rests firmly on "actualities far more pervasive than, say, the gaiety of the troubled 1890s." The decade experienced "a fundamental shift in American moral and religious attitudes."[10] Some of the personal and social implications of this radical shift in the contextual teaching of the commandment against adultery can be sketched out here.

Early in 1960, Vance Packard decided to study the changing sexual climate in America. Expecting to complete his survey in a year or so, Professor Packard devoted five years to the task. His voluminous work documents not only the great moral revolution but the sexual wilderness it left in its wake. Yesterday's proven guides had been wiped out. No single code of morality claimed majority support in American society. Millions of Americans roamed anxiously in a wilderness that alternately attracted and repelled them.

This was new in Western social experience.[11] From the Reformation to the end of the nineteenth century, Protestant Europe and Protestant America were convinced—and impressed their conviction on their children—that chastity before marriage and fidelity in marriage are personally wholesome and socially necessary. Catholic society agreed, adding its own proviso that any interference with procreation is immoral. That was yesterday. Today, this brand of morality is spurned, ignored, or seriously questioned by most Americans. In his novel *Marry Me,* John Updike has Jerry, involved in an affair with his friend's wife Sally, say that it was happening "in the twilight of the old morality . . . there's just enough to torment us and not enough to hold us in." At least five current views on sex in America—other than wholesome sex in secure, relational marriages—can be identified clearly, each representing a substantial bloc of subscribers.

First, millions of Americans still cling to Victorian morality, some neurotically. These people—many of whom are mechanical, unhappy, and hypocritical in their sexuality—are, in many cases, sex-starved humans condemned to live in a sex-saturated society. Many experiment with sex angrily, coyly, manipulatively. Rigid and guilt-ridden, these harassed people seek desperately to break out of their sexual prisons through conscious and unconscious acts of rebellion against an inherited Victorian sexual life-style that they rightly sense is not human.[12]

Second, increasing numbers of Americans subscribe to a utilitarian sex ethic. "Sex for kicks" is not only popular among high school and college students, it is also popular among many married couples. A young matron has an extramarital affair because she is bored with suburban life. A middle-aged executive initiates an extramarital relationship because his work has gone flat. A couple, dissatisfied with their sex life, agree to swap mates with another couple. Harold Robbins and the late Jacqueline Susann became wealthy describing this style of open sex. But it is not new. It rests on an old doctrine and an older practice. Mechanically oriented and biologically motivated, sex without passion is dehumanizing.

Third, "recreational sex" has hundreds of thousands of devotees in our society. This view asserts that sex exists primarily for pleasure. Sex is a compartmentalized human activity to be "enjoyed" without personal involvement or personal responsibility. *Playboy* magazine popularized this view in the 1960s; it is the ancient philosophy of hedonism. Providing six million moderns with vicarious excitement (playmate of the month) and emboldening some to find their own playmates, Hefner made enough money to furnish an expensive pad, purchase a jet, and invest heavily in Bunny Clubs.

But recreational sex is also dehumanizing. Separating pleasure from purpose and personal commitment from personal responsibility, it robs both partners of their *human* sexuality. Lucy Komisar, active in the Women's Liberation Movement in the early 1970s, writes: "Feminists also protest the general male proclivity to regard us as decorative, amusing sex objects even in the world outside bed. We resent the sexual sell in advertising, the catcalls we get on the street, girlie magazines and pornography. . . . Even the supposedly humanistic worlds of rock music and radical politics are not very different. Young girls who join 'the scene' or the 'movement' are labeled 'groupies' and are sexually exploited."[13] Lynette "Squeaky" Fromme, a follower of Charles Manson and would-be assassin of President Ford in 1975, is a dramatic example of such exploitation. Rollo May provides this sobering criticism of recreational sex.

Playboy has indeed caught on to something significant in American society: Cox believes it to be "the repressed fear of involvement with women." I go farther and hold that it, as an example of the new puritanism, gets its dynamic from a repressed anxiety in American men that underlies even the fear of involvement. This is the repressed anxiety about impotence. Everything in the magazine is beautifully concocted to bolster the *illusion of potency* without ever putting it to the test or challenge at all. Noninvolvement (like playing it cool) is elevated into the ideal model for the Playboy. This is possible because the illusion is air-tight, ministering as it does to men fearful for their potency, and capitalizing on this anxiety.[14]

A fourth attitude toward sex in our society rests on what Joseph Fletcher identifies broadly as "situation ethics." This view, which insists on personal responsibility, suggests that each person must evaluate each situation as it occurs. But Fletcher, rejecting the law absolutely, is too flexible for many.[15] This view differs radically from the other contemporary views on sex because it seeks to take each situation seriously and calls for love as the only norm. Consciously, the practitioners of this view are not utilitarian; they do not consciously seek selfish gratification; they aim to relate as persons. Sex is unthinkable for them unless they love each other. The dangers in this approach are obvious. The "situation" *and* "love as the norm" can be treacherous guides. Reliance on either or both without objective points of reference can injure others and cause pain to the practitioners.

This attitude toward sex poses several stubborn questions. Who is capable of unselfish love? Who is altogether free from neurotic tendencies? Whose finite mind can judge the complex consequences of any human act, especially for the next generation? Who can make judgments that are equally good for *all* persons affected by any man-woman sexual relationship? A durable regard for persons and the mature acceptance

91

of social responsibility are casualties in this currently popular view of sex. Nonetheless, many university and military chaplains, parish pastors, and secular counselors approve it.[16] Reporting on the seventy-sixth American Booksellers Convention, William Cole mentions in passing the titles of three new books that reflect America's irresponsible value system: among them is a book for unmarried couples living together.[17] The moral revolution of the 1960s has indeed altered the life-styles of millions of couples in the 1970s.

Fifth, there is the homosexual style among males and females. Other peoples in other cultures and other nations have accepted this sex style for centuries. Americans, like their British cousins, have not. Our society has been secretive, suspicious, and condemnatory of homosexuality until a decade or so ago. During the 1960s, a human desire to understand the homosexual emerged in some quarters. The change in the moral climate is readily discernible. Two decades ago, actors of stature, like Rex Harrison and Richard Burton, would have refused to portray two aging homosexuals as they did in a motion picture that attracted millions of viewers in 1969. Films like *The Fox, The Killing of Sister George, The Boys in the Band, Staircase, The Midnight Rider,* and *Midnight Cowboy* could not have been produced in the 1950s. American opinion has undergone a radical change in its attitude toward homosexuals. On October 31, 1969, *Time* magazine gave its cover story to the gay society. Even so, the climate has changed slowly. The tragic biography of the 1920s tennis superstar Big Bill Tilden, ruined because of his homosexual activities, could not be published until 1976.

The debate turns on whether homosexuality is a disease to be treated or a way of life among consenting adults that society should accept. Christian and secular counselors differ on this, but they, like others, appreciate the new openness, candor, and compassionate concern toward homosexuals as persons.[18]

Fashioning a Stable Society

By the mid-1960s, teen-agers, young people, and many of their parents were wandering, confused and frightened, in a sexual wilderness. More and more people were admitting that they were lost, and millions more revealed their "lostness" in scores of neurotic ways. Mechanical sex, utilitarian sex, recreational sex, situational sex, and homosexuality had claimed millions of Americans who were engaging in more sex, more freely and openly, but appearing to enjoy it less. For many Americans, sex was turning out to be more of a problem than a fulfilling, joyous human experience.

During the 1950s, Pitrim Sorkin, a Harvard sociologist, concluded that the change in American sex mores had set the stage for a "listless drift toward sex anarchy." A decade later, Vance Packard documented that man-woman relationships in America had produced "a sexual wilderness." In 1969, Rollo May was discussing the new puritanism in sexual attitudes and practices.

I define this puritanism as consisting of three elements. First, *a state of alienation from the body*. Second, *the separation of emotion from reason*. And third, *the use of the body as a machine*. . . . Thus it is not surprising that, as sex becomes more machinelike, with passion irrelevant and then even pleasure diminishing, the problem has come full circle. And we find, *mirabile dictu*, a progression from an *anesthetic* attitude to an *antiseptic* one. Sexual contact itself then tends to get put on the shelf and to be avoided. This is another and surely least constructive aspect of the new puritanism; it returns, finally, to a new asceticism. This is said graphically in a charming limerick that seems to have sprung up on some sophisticated campus:

> The word has come down from the Dean
> That with the aid of the teaching machine,
> King Oedipus Rex
> Could have learned about sex
> Without ever touching the Queen[19]

Leslie Farber makes the same point in his critical essay on the work of Masters and Johnson.[20] Jacqueline Susann's book

93

The Love Machine was a best seller and major motion picture. The characters in Peter DeVries' book *I Hear America Swinging* were appraised by one reviewer as "a motley band of professional bumpkins, homespun sages, and rubes, one of whom, Artie Pringel, finds promiscuity a 'kind of discipline, a challenging call to arms—anybody's.'"[21] By the late 1970s, sex had become for many a biological sport, machinelike, dull, inhuman.

The commandment against adultery was designed originally for people who were behaving sexually as millions of people are behaving today. Moses' band of liberated slaves were undisciplined on all fronts. God reminded them that they could not build a secure nation until they accepted marriage as a public institution as well as a private relationship. Sexual morality was also loose in Jesus' day. He called his contemporaries "an adulterous generation" (Matthew 12). Paul, too, gave detailed attention to the widespread sexual abuses in the new Christian communities, especially the church in Corinth (I Corinthians).

The sexual revolution in America in the 1960s has produced a climate that rejects values and avoids personal discipline in sexual relationships. By the mid-1970s, sex had become an end in itself for many American men and women. The current preoccupation in many communities with "bedroom olympics" suggests a deepening fault in the social psyche itself. Sex has been separated from intimate commitment for millions of persons in and outside legal marriage[22] Perhaps no people, the Romans included, idolized sex more than contemporary Americans. They look to it as a means of salvation rather than as a wholesome, joyous, often humorous strand in a fulfilling permanent man-woman (human) relationship based on commitment, fidelity, communication, and public declaration. The separation of sex from passion and commitment and love weakens the moral fabric of our society and—linked with other dehumanizing forces in our technological society—

endorses and supports an American culture that robs life of its God-intended meaning.

Marriage is indeed a private affair—intimate, exciting, joyous, maturing, frustrating, fulfilling. But it is also a public institution, a pillar in a stable society. Persons who marry must accept the relationship as a joint commitment, face reality, and accept God's authority in their homes—including their bedrooms—or they will not be able to face other persons in society with openness, candor, humor, integrity, realism, and compassion.

When fidelity does not permeate the marriage relationship, and professional counseling has not helped, divorce may be the lesser evil for the partners—and their children—than their continuing in a devious or hostile marriage. Not all marriages are ordained by God; many are entered into because of emotional immaturity, to escape from an unpleasant parent-home situation, or through artful manipulation bent on self-destruction. The sooner these unpromising unions are addressed in candor and with compassion in the context of professional counseling—and dissolved wherever reconciliation proves to be impossible—the better it will be for the partners and the children. The commandment "Do not commit adultery" is a personal and social corrective and guide in an era when sex—separated from passion, commitment, responsibility, and love—is viewed as an end in itself, an activity that is no longer human for many.

There is also a deeper strand of life-experience that this commandment, read in Christian context, brings to the surface. It concerns the person, married or unmarried, who looks on any other person, including his or her mate, with lust in the heart: Jesus says *that* person is guilty of adultery. His absolute demand brings every human, however faithful in his or her commitments, under God's judgment, placing each in continuing need of God's grace. That is of the earth, earthy, for each creature must examine his or her love in the light of

95

God's love if each is to be for the other rather than for self.

Commandments five, six, and seven are essential for establishing a stable society, creating a humane community, and providing guidelines for authentic family living. "Do not kill." Anyone who is angry with another without cause is guilty of murder. "Do not steal." Anyone who declines to take up the burdens of others murders their spirit. "Do not commit adultery." Whoever looks lustfully on another in his or her heart is guilty of adultery. In the present climate of libertinism and social irresponsibility, when each does what he or she wants to do without regard for others, these three commandments are the new morality.

We shall consider another strand in that morality in the next chapter.

CHAPTER V

ON BEING FREE TO APPRECIATE OTHERS

Do not covet; do not envy.

Wholesome human relationships rest on integrity. That is obvious. The desire to know the truth, tell it compassionately, and follow it resolutely are proofs of that integrity. That is not obvious. The desire to know, tell, and do the truth is warped by covetousness, greed, and jealousy. These sins of the spirit distort rationality, blur perceptions of truth, and create barriers between ourselves and other selves. Like "the three faces of Eve," covetousness, greed, and jealousy are the three ugly faces of envy. And envy is the mate of pride.

The deadly effects of envy are not always evident even to professional counselors, philosophers, and theologians. There are mountains of in-depth studies on pride. There are few serious treatments of envy anywhere in theological, philosophical, or psychological literature. Leslie H. Farber, an earlier astute observer of society, comments on this lack.

The protean character of envy and its talent for disguise account, I believe, for the infrequency of studies on the subject. Because of the variety of forms it may take, it is often simply impossible to recognize. This is true, not only for the observer, who by definition must be more gullible about such a subjective state as envy, but also for the envious one himself, whose rational powers may lend almost unholy assistance to the need for self-deception.[1]

Envy feeds our ego-centeredness. It imprisons us in self-absorption. It destroys our capacity to appreciate other persons. Allowed to roam unchecked in our imagination, envy can turn one into a self-centered person like novelist Edith Wharton, who was described by a contemporary: "Edith is a little country bounded on the north, east, south, and west by Edith."

Commandments nine and ten focus on envy. They warn against coveting openly or secretly any*one* who is committed to another (wife, husband, child, friend, employer) or any*thing* that belongs to anybody else (job, house, farm, car, reputation). But covetousness, like greed and jealousy, roots in envy. Envy alienates one from God, self, and other persons. It does greater damage to the practitioner than the victim. In the first century, Horace wrote that "Sicilian tyrants never invented a greater term than envy." Richard Sheridan observed in the eighteenth century that "there is not a passion so strongly rooted in the human heart as envy." Thomas Hobbes wrote that "the praise of ancient authors precedes not from the reverence of the dead, but from . . . envy of the living."

Envy is a vicious, stubborn, Hydra-headed monster. For envy, Cain murdered Abel. For envy, Saul tried to kill David. For envy, the Pharisees railroaded Jesus to the cross. For envy, Paul boasted about his discipleship. To be human is to envy. Francis Bacon observed in the fifteenth century that only death can "extinguish envy." Envy is a demon that lays waste to life.

The two commandments against envy turn us full circle. The first three commandments focus on our personal-corporate relationships with God. The next five focus on our relationships with other persons in his family, on our personal and social responsibilities. These commandments focus on our *attitudes* toward other persons. They are unique. Their predecessors deal with specific actions, but these two forbid a state of mind. They call us to appreciate and value the unique gifts of other persons. They invite us to search the inner recesses of our being; to examine our passions, our deepest desires, and our fickle loyalties to our own human potential, to true neighborliness, to God. Right desires, shaped by grace, foster good deeds. Wholesome desires set us free to relate openly to others, because we can then enjoy and appreciate their talents. So these commandments turn us full circle: back to God who alone can cleanse and renew the inner person.

This dual commandment strikes directly at the sin of the spirit—pride. Christians know that of all the sins that root in pride, envy is the most ferocious. The sins of the flesh are identifiable, uncouth, hurtful. The sins of the spirit are elusive, destructive, demonic. The admonition against covetousness brings us face to face with these intertwined sins of the spirit: envy, avarice, greed, jealousy, vainglory. Outside God's love, this dual commandment hardens our hearts or drives us to despair. It is human to covet. The only differences among us lie in the degrees of our envy and in our ability to hide envy from ourselves and others. Lovers of self, we begrudge others their good fortune, especially when our fortunes are running low. Envy feeds our prejudices, distorts our judgments, destroys our peace of mind.

Envy respects no person, class, ethnic group, race, or nation. All humans are its victims. The Nazis coveted Czechoslovakia's territory. The American colonists coveted the land of the American Indians. The Israelis covet a strip of Arab territory. The Arabs covet the Israelis' military capability. The Western world covets the Arabs' oil. The Third World covets the Western world's affluence, technology, and power. Chief among the multiple causes of war are envy, covetousness, and greed.

Covetousness is rampant in America. We covet one another's mates, children, jobs, houses, cars, clothes, education, culture. Women envy men their favored places in business, industry, and politics, while more and more men, coveting their own favored positions, are becoming meanly defensive toward women. The dispossessed want what the affluent enjoy, and the affluent dig in greedily to keep what they possess. American political parties have played to this human sin from the beginning of the Republic. Jefferson and Jackson and Roosevelt were not less guilty in exploiting human envy than Grant and Hoover and Nixon. The American Revolution was a mean-spirited civil war in which covetousness, envy, and greed were mixed with love of liberty, concern for justice, and hope for a republican political society.

The alienating power of envy comes into hard focus when we examine it intimately. Some who were bitterly opposed to the election of John Kennedy in 1960 honestly feared his religion while others honestly feared his "liberalism." Many, however, attacked him from pure envy. They coveted his wealth, intelligence, wit, style, charisma, wife, and children. But few faced up to that then, and few have done so since. Roosevelt, too, in another crisis period, was the victim of envious attacks. Both presidents were human; neither was a demigod. Many of their supporters knew that when they voted for them. The usual posthumous revelations—like the revelations about Washington and Lincoln and Wilson—did not surprise or shock those who had neither deified nor envied them. But many who envied Kennedy in life are still carping at him in death. Envy, jealousy, guilt, bitterness, meanspiritedness, and self-righteousness are common *human* frailties.

Let the focus be widened at the person-to-person level of human experience. Scientists, for example, are not immune to envy. Robert Oppenheimer's distinguished career was ended abruptly and his character vilified in the mid-1950s more through professional jealousy than ideological differences.[2] Envy, like the common cold, ravages medical doctors and truckers, lawyers and file clerks, teachers and children, executives and secretaries, clergy and lay persons. Many congregations are victimized by envy, especially those fighting to survive institutionally. Nonetheless, envy is the sin that the clergy and laity do not talk about, because they will not face up to it. This suggests that segments of the church do not take sin seriously or rely expectantly on God's grace.

Authors are particularly vulnerable to envy. F. Scott Fitzgerald could not accept that his literary star was falling as Ernest Hemingway's star was rising. In time, the aging Hemingway came to envy the young Hemingway. William Faulkner appears to have been free of envy. He wrote, he said, to make money; he had two families and many relatives to support. He never read reviews of his books!

Leslie Farber speaks with candor and insight about his envy of the eminent psychiatrist, Harry Stack Sullivan.

I remember with some clarity the first time I heard Harry Stack Sullivan lecture. His subject matter escapes me now as it escaped me then, but how well I recall him fussing with the recording apparatus. As I later explained to a friend, I was appalled that such a respected figure in our profession could so nakedly address himself to posterity. Wanting, of course, to give my friend a wholly objective picture of the occasion, I went on to depict Sullivan's affectations of manner and phraseology, always careful to preface each objective statement with some generous remark such as: 'Don't think me envious because I know this man to be a genius in the field of psychiatry. So it is doubly unfortunate;' and so on. The example is as crude as my envy was strong. Inasmuch as envy rendered me impervious to the content of his lecture, the object of my disparagement, it will be noted, was his personal style. What I clearly observed in that style was his egotism, his infatuation with self, his dramatic need to impress that self on both posterity and on his more immediate audience. In brief, envy took the form of disparagement. But what of

101

my own self-assertion? Certainly, to my friend, I dissembled the degree to which I was at a loss at this particular lecture and concealed the misery and stupidity fostered by my envy, which prevented me from giving him any idea of what Sullivan had said. Instead, I asserted myself brashly and authoritatively, if unhappily, representing a confidence in my own abilities that was, at that moment, as necessary as it was undeserved.[3]

Webster's definition of envy provides a strong base for an understanding of envy and its multiple threats to personal and social health: "chagrin or discontent at the excellence or good fortune of another." Three decades ago, a Catholic priest whose name I cannot recall, described envy as "sorrow at the other person's good fortune." That description is especially insightful—and rugged. It does not accept envy simply as an irritating reality in personal and social life, a peripheral inconvenience in daily living. It sees envy for what it really is: a vicious sin of the spirit that breeds multiple evil effects in persons and society. Shakespeare's Iago, speaking of Othello, provides us with a description of envy that is sharper than the clearest definition or a dozen case studies:

> He hath a daily beauty in his life
> That makes me ugly. . . .
>
> O! beware, my lord, of jealousy;
> It is the green-eyed monster which doth mock
> The meat it feeds on.

Jean Jacques Rousseau, influential French philosopher of the eighteenth century, describes with raw honesty a harsh personal-social consequence of envy: "I pretended to despise what I could not emulate."

Countless sorrows burden us at one time or another, but the sorrow bred by envy haunts some people all the time and all people some of the time. But how does one get at this sin of the spirit? How does one root an attitude out of one's mind? How does one cope with envy?

On Being Free to Appreciate Others

The deep issues of life originate in the heart, the human imagination. First come the desires, conscious and unconscious; next, the decisions, calculated and spontaneous; finally, the deeds, well-directed and impulsive. So Paul, centuries after Moses, urged the scattered Christian communities, not yet institutionalized, to "sorrow with those who sorrow and to rejoice with those who rejoice." The first part of his exhortation calls for sensitivity and compassion; the second, alerting us to covetousness, encourages us to rely on God's grace. Decent people are sensitive to others in need; they sorrow with those who sorrow, however briefly or superficially. But few enter eagerly and fully into their neighbor's joy.

The Father, warning his children against envy, goes to the wellsprings of life: human desire. Jesus taught that as men and women think in their hearts (imagination), so are they. Desire fosters the deed. Our Redeemer liberates us from wrong desires. He alone can cleanse our hearts and purify our imaginations. So we pray, "Create in us, O Lord, clean desires." We pray, "Let the thoughts in our hearts be acceptable in your sight." Otherwise, we shall be driven to despair by this commandment—and sink ever deeper into an envious spirit.

Specifically, this dual commandment admonishes us against coveting overtly or covertly another's mate, child, friend, job, reputation, or material holdings (land, industries, cities, oil, zinc, etc.). We are admonished against wanting inordinately—which is to risk trying to get one way or another or saddening ourselves daily over not possessing—whatever belongs to another person, group, class, race, institution, or nation.

When we want passionately what belongs to another—and allow ourselves to want it long enough—our disposition to act on that secret desire usually gets out of hand. Recall the romance between King Edward VIII and Wallis Warfield

Simpson in the mid-1930s, which stirred depression-ridden Britain and America. Most Britons, like their cousins in America and neighbors in France, supported Edward's selfish demand that British tradition and Anglican church law be scuttled to allow the twice-married Baltimore belle to be his queen. That did not occur. British tradition and the Anglican Church held firm. Archbishop of Canterbury William Temple declared bluntly that the controversy could have been avoided had Edward terminated his relationship with Mrs. Simpson when he discovered that he was falling in love with another man's wife. Covetousness is a smoldering fire; unquenched, it rages destructively. Another king, David, also demonstrated three millenia earlier the evil in coveting another man's wife, Bathsheba. The contemporary cry "What I want" means that one's personal gratification is valued above one's personal obligation to others and to one's own authentic self.

This dual commandment admonishes us—when envy rears its head—to strike it dead, eliminate its cause, or contain it. Martin Luther said he could not prevent the birds from flying over his head, but he could keep them from making a nest in his hair. Specifically, he was speaking of anxieties, but his sane observation is also applicable here. Out of the imagination (heart) come the issues of life. To covet what isn't ours—and not to discipline ourselves—is to risk acting on an illicit desire that will hurt us and others. This commandment is intensely practical: don't play with fire; extinguish the flame or get out of the building!

Covetousness corrodes the human spirit and despoils human relationships. Whenever one wallows in envy over another's talent, one cannot enjoy the fruits of that person's talent. Whenever one indulges his envy of another's good fortune, one cannot share in the joy of it. The prodigal's brother was like that. He would be at home in our society. Male and female chauvinism are multi-rooted sins against personhood—one's own and others, but often the taproot is envy rather than cultural inequities. Many marriage relationships are tarnished and diminished because one partner envies, usually covertly and unconsciously, the personal gifts of the other; he or she cannot rejoice in the other's good fortune. In American families the relationship between parents and children is often warped, because many parents envy their children's youth, attractiveness, imagination, intellect, or opportunities. It is also true that some children envy the talents and competence of their parents (a son his father's business success; a daughter her mother's beauty) preventing thereby the growth of wholesome relationships between them. Envy despoils human relationships.

Whenever we envy the competence of another, we cut ourselves off from learning from that person. Whenever we envy the accomplishments of another, we set up a barrier between that person and ourselves. Whenever we envy the talents of another, we are tempted to bear false witness against that person and we always succumb, if not in word and deed, then in thought. The attack may take the polite form of declining to acknowledge the other's accomplishments or the crass form of mean detraction. Many full-time church workers are badly warped by envy. It is a giant adversary that pins some strong Christians to the ground, preventing their solid personal growth toward freedom. Envy lets loose its demons in every generation, but it may be the chief sin of the spirit in our affluent, success-dominated, money-oriented American culture.

We *are* burdened with envy. Few of us are able to accept a compliment gracefully; we are suspicious of others' motives. Two psychiatrists in different parts of the country, each commenting on this phenomenon, said without knowledge of the other's view that this is true because most people are so envious of others that they do not trust what any other person says. Both psychiatrists also observed that contemporary American culture incites and nurtures envy. They judged that ours is the most acquisitive and suspicious culture in human history. Recall the fierce acquisitiveness and deepening suspicions (bordering on paranoia) that characterized the administrations of former presidents Johnson and Nixon.[4] Both men came up the hard way; success-driven, they were products of our culture.

Western culture in general and American culture in particular incites envy, encourages acquisitiveness, breeds suspicion, spawns frustration, and induces loneliness. So, people protect themselves reflexively. They offer smooth compliments to avoid serious conversation, to escape in-depth relationships, and to manipulate other persons. A large strand in this breach in human relationships is sorrow at another's good fortune. This meanspiritedness denies us and others the satisfactions of wholesome, secure human relationships. Envy corrodes and maims—and, if persisted in, destroys— our human capacity to experience life fully. A host of people sink slowly into the quagmire of their envy. Consequently, the harm envy does to other persons and to our social fabric is incalculable.

Covetousness also stunts our growth as persons because it dulls our social sensibilities. Jesus' unforgettable story of the well-to-do farmer who built new barns only to die impoverished in spirit—deprived of solid relationships with God and other persons—reveals the cancer of covetousness (Luke 12:13-21). America is the most affluent nation in history, yet most people want more and more money, goods, pleasure, and comfort. Affluence breeds acquisitiveness. Like the rich farmer, we too go after more than we really need.

This complex, ambiguous problem is not easy to resolve. We Americans are in effect caught in a web of our own weaving. It is human creativity that produces, invents, and improves our material situation. So the temptations to covet in an affluent society escalate with every new material improvement. In *Culture Against Man*, Jules Henry argues that the first two commandments in American society are "Create more desire" and "Thou shalt consume." Observe this inevitable sequence of events. In 1908, the person with a horse and carriage wanted a Model-T Ford. Human technology had invented and was marketing the horseless carriage. In 1937, a teen-ager would want his father's Packard for dating. His son, in turn, would lobby for the classic two-seat Jaguar. And his grandson would want his own car *and* a motorcycle *and* a snowmobile! Airlines advertise their cuisines, autos their size, motels their luxury, and churches their air-conditioning! The battle against envy is external as well as internal, cultural as well as spiritual. Create more desire; we must consume. Our culture has produced an anthropology based on envy: if man is to be man, he must be a consumer. We must attack envy, therefore, in both the private and public spheres. It plays a larger role in socioeconomic and political decisions than people generally realize. Our spiritual health affects our national economy directly and indirectly.

There are actions that we can take to limit and control covetousness. We can, as we noted above, keep on the alert for signs of greed in our interpersonal and vocational relationships. We can pray for right desires and cultivate them. Covetousness is a demon that goes down only after much prayer and self-discipline. We can also alert ourselves to and stand against the social climate that enlarges envy's power over us. At the polls we can choose those representatives who seek seriously to initiate far-reaching tax reforms that will balance the awesome disparities between those who have and those who have not. Through alert, responsible political representatives we can express our criticisms of multinational corporations when they act against human interests anywhere; we can monitor the military-industrial complex and bureaucratic government. Some citizens' lobbies against bureaucratic government promise change. We can support them and act through them. We can, as many people in Christian congregations do, contribute money in a disciplined way to responsible charitable causes. We can worship every Sunday because that disciplined and glad act livens our sensibilities to God, self, and others. More intimately, we can examine critically our personal life-styles and simplify them substantially. We who are church members can enlarge our support of Christ's ministry in and to the world by giving up some things that we have been claiming as our right yet have not really needed at all. Clerical and lay leaders in the congregations can call the members in specific ways to decide daily for character above comfort, conscience above convenience, service above self—having first done so themselves. Adapting a simpler life-style will partially free us from the tyranny of things. It will encourage us to concentrate more on persons than on possessions. It will bring aid, comfort, and hope to the dispossessed.

The Lord of covenant law warns against envy because it maims persons, destroys human relationships, spawns loneliness, sets class against class and nation against nation, and divides the world into the "haves" and "have nots." Envy is the elusive sin that adopts more disguises than a summer-stock player on the straw-hat circuit. It is harder to kill than a snake. Envy, Leslie Farber observes, tends toward diffusion, feeds on itself, has a talent for disguising itself (covetousness, jealousy, greed, unbridled self-assertiveness, ingratiating behavior, uncritical praise). "I am convinced," Dr. Farber writes, "that the envious man is miserable, even though what he knowingly feels is not envy but perplexing pain."

Envy reflects every human's ingrained disposition to put the self forward, to push God off center stage, to install the ego on a makeshift throne. It is a structural fault in mankind's nature to despoil our *true* humanity. We roll in the mud, stick our noses in our neighbor's business, cast an envious eye on what belongs to another, use power for our own ends, burn our enemy's cities and our own, pollute our air, and ravage our own and others' countrysides. But there are also occasions when we demonstrate an amazing concern for others: we take heroic positions, give beyond our means, lay down our lives for friends and/or our principles.[5] We criticize our young unmercifully yet sacrifice to educate them. We invent and use nuclear and napalm bombs while working sporadically for a stable international order. Blaise Pascal provides a classic description of this schizoid fault in humanity: "What a chimera then is man, what a novelty, what a monster, what chaos, what a subject of contradiction, what a prodigy; judge of all things, yet an imbecile earthworm; depository of truth, yet a sewer of uncertainty and error; pride and refuse of the universe."[6]

Human life is a mosaic of failure and achievement, frustration and satisfaction, misery and grandeur. No one can be certain what one will be in any particular moment or do in any concrete situation. This innate instability and unpredictability is complicated further by the social dynamics set in motion by other unpredictable selves. Society both unsettles and steadies us. One demon that dwarfs us all and disrupts society is envy. To detect it in its many disguises is a step toward personal freedom. To wrestle with it seriously is to learn firsthand that we need help beyond our own. This final commandment can lead us to grace.

We also need to ask if there is anything we should covet, want inordinately, hunger and thirst after. From Genesis to Revelation—and on every front in contemporary society—we are reminded that we should want others to have adequate food, shelter, clothing, and a fair share of life's comforts even as we want them for ourselves. It is a perversion of biblical Christianity to spiritualize material needs. Humans are not disembodied spirits, "souls with ears." The medievalists were so successful in disembodying man that it required the Reformation, the Counter-Reformation, the Renaissance, the Age of Discovery, and the Industrial Revolution to shatter their narrow, depressing views on life. Marxism, challenging the medieval cultural perversion of Christianity, is a Christian heresy. Jesus did not minimize the material side of life. He was not an ascetic. He enjoyed good food and wine. He appreciated decent housing. He coveted the loyalty of his friends. In our day, Jesus may well have appreciated the Russian ballet, a symphony concert under Sir Thomas Beecham's direction, the Smithsonian Institute, the Louvre, a play like *A Man for All Seasons*, a movie like *In the Heat of the Night*, a novel like *A Tale of Two Cities*. He taught plainly that the material things of this world are given by God for human enjoyment and personal enrichment. Jesus showed a special concern for the materially poor as well as for the poor in spirit. But he did not accept poverty and social injustice as ineradicable aspects of human life. He taught that the earth's goods should be shared fairly. God expects us to want for ourselves and others the right to work to meet necessary human needs.

God also expects us to covet for ourselves and others the opportunities to develop the talents he has placed in his human creation. In God's family, there is no separate but equal education, no second sex, no hierarchical marriage, no white man's burden, no bureaucratic community of believers. Those are human inventions inspired by the devil. God calls us to be responsible for other persons, classes, nations, and races, because he welcomes all people into his family. He expects us to covet opportunities for all people to develop the talents he has given them. That is galling for the labor unions, management, the medical profession, ethnic groups, the church—everyone. Each person and group, with varying intensity, works for its own interests and guards jealously its own rights. Each leans strongly to being an exclusive club preoccupied with catering to its members' self-interest.

Third, God expects us to covet spiritual gifts—that is, want them inordinately. Jesus defined that high expectation winsomely but plainly:

On Being Free to Appreciate Others

Blessed are the poor in spirit, for theirs is the kingdom of heaven.
Blessed are those who mourn, for they shall be comforted.
Blessed are the meek, for they shall inherit the earth.
Blessed are those who hunger and thirst for righteousness, for they
shall be satisfied.
Blessed are the merciful, for they shall obtain mercy.
Blessed are the pure in heart, for they shall see God.
Blessed are the peacemakers, for they shall be called sons of God.
Blessed are those who are persecuted for righteousness' sake, for
theirs is the kingdom of heaven.
Blessed are you when men revile you and persecute you and utter all
kinds of evil against you falsely on my account.
Rejoice and be glad, for your reward is great in heaven.

(Matthew 5:3-10)

Jesus valued the natural world, subhuman creatures, and all
material aspects of God's creation. And he loved life. Bertrand
Russell announced privately a few months before his death, "I
hate to leave this world." So did Jesus at Gethsemane, but he
loved God more. He kept his priorities straight even under the
pressure of the cross. He said that we should respond first to
the need of the inner person to pursue truth, beauty,
justice—God. When one's personal wants and desires are
ordered by God's grace, liberation in this life and fulfillment
in eternity come. So Paul pleaded with the early church
to give its heart and mind in the pursuit of the good,
the true, the beautiful, the lovely, and the just. All of us
are called to want inordinately, to covet, for ourselves
and others the gifts of the spirit.

Let it be said again: the negative and positive addressments
inherent in the last two commandments can drive sensitive
persons to despair. They can turn us against God if we see him
as a police officer. They can alienate us from him unless we
discern that the God who demands first place in our lives is
the same God who wants to free us, and can, from the sins of
the spirit and the flesh when we accept his authority and, in
his strength, do his commandments. It is he who showers us
with the riches of the gospel. It is his Spirit that joins us to

Christ. It is his Son who frees us. The riches of God are open to everyone; each need only claim them and serve his neighbor. God promises to establish his law in our inward being, to write it on our hearts, to make us co-laborers with his Son. That is the miracle of Christianity—God's Spirit refashions human spirits to will what he wills, to have the mind of Christ. So the Christian lays great store on the "commands with promise" and on obedience in freedom.

Christians—restrained, corrected, guided, and measured by the commandments—pray daily, "Create in me a clean heart and renew a right spirit within me." And God does. They pray, "Let the thoughts of our hearts be acceptable in your sight." And God does. We discover that we are empowered by him to liberate others. Paul called that "Christ appealing by me." We discover that God's commands are not too hard for us, because every child of God is able to defeat the world. This is how we win the victory over the world: with "our faith" (I John 5:3-4).

One man brought freedom and discipline into equilibrium. In so doing, he set us free to do that too—in his company. That is the theme of the next chapter.

CHAPTER VI

HOW ONE MAN GOT FREEDOM AND DISCIPLINE IN BALANCE

Millions of people inside and outside the church recognize the need for broad moral absolutes, for norms, for fixed points of reference in decision-making. They know that life without externally defined boundaries and internal disciplines goes stale and that society without norms goes to pieces or turns to fascism. A boy's summer camp without any rules or regulations would be bedlam. Professional football without rules, umpires, linemen, and referees would be mayhem. The carnage on our highways would be horrendous if all traffic laws were suspended and all police patrols were recalled. Without civil and criminal laws enforced promptly and fairly, the state's power to protect human life and property would collapse. Life without law is unthinkable.

That is also true in authentic Christian experience: the promises of God carry his demands. But has any human being ever fulfilled the whole will of God? What happens to a person who takes God's moral law as an absolute requirement in a world like ours? Reinhold Niebuhr, scarred by his jousts for economic justice in industrial Detroit after the First World War, wrote *Moral Man and Immoral Society* in which he argued that the efforts of the best-intentioned people are blunted, deflected, often defeated by an immoral social order. Examples of this reality are many.

Three courageous Germans—Goerdler, von Stauffenberg, and Bonhoeffer—were executed for their active parts in the 1944 bomb plot on Hitler's life. All three violated the fifth commandment, having judged that Hitler had suspended all the commandments in forging and maintaining the Nazi State. The ambiguities of history press in. Were Goerdler (a Jew), von Stauffenberg (a Catholic), and Bonhoeffer (a Lutheran clergyman) political martyrs or religious martyrs? Did Pope Pius XII, Christ's "vicar on earth," fracture the moral law of God when he declined to speak out firmly against the Nazi's genocide against the Jews in Europe because he wanted to keep the institutional Roman Church intact? Sir Thomas More, a man of grace and high personal morality, took a radically different stance against King Henry VIII (who wanted to sever his ties with Rome so that he could divorce his wife), losing his head on the chopping block in the Tower of London for his opposition. Which of these men, if any, was maturely Christian? Certainly, the motives of none were wholly Christian.

Historians agree that Thomas Jefferson brought to the American presidency the ablest intellect and that Abraham Lincoln brought to that office the highest moral character. Yet, Lincoln, the man who called the nation to bind up its wounds "with firmness in the right, as God gives us to see the right," used the moral issue of slavery as a political instrument, suspended the writ of habeus corpus, and directed total war against the South in 1864 and 1865.

It appears that no human being in the course of recorded history has been or is able to keep the whole moral law of God. Each has a private and a public ethic that do not mesh neatly, and sometimes do not mesh at all. As Reinhold Niebuhr stated, "Man's capacity for justice makes democracy possible; but man's inclination to injustice makes democracy necessary." Responsible humanists argue, and rightly, that truth is better than falsehood, fidelity and grace are better in marriage and friendship and politics than infidelity and meanness, that environmental responsibility is rational behavior, that the quest for social justice is sane behavior, and that intelligent resistance to the ways that lead to war (arms race, nuclear proliferation, economic injustice) is proof of our humanity. Human performance in all these areas, however, falls short of the humanist's idealistic hopes. Human beings are neither wholly nor consistently moral in private or in public.

But suppose one human being, one mortal, one in the species called *homo sapiens,* did keep the whole moral law of God. Suppose some mother's child—bone of our bone, sinew of our sinew, flesh of our flesh—did God's will fully in the world's harsh arena where we humans live and die, love and hate, hope and despair, and never do God's will more than piecemeal. Suppose that a man, burdened by our human infirmities, not only fulfilled the whole moral law of God and offered himself as an example, but was also raised up again by God, with whom he lived in the perfect union of obedience and love, making him a presence in every generation, everyone's contemporary, so that all humans can grow in doing God's will too.

That is a solid strand in the wonderful story the early Christians heralded around the Roman world.[1] They proclaimed that Jesus, Son of God and Son of man, had done for all of us what we could not do for ourselves or for others: that Jesus of Nazareth had fulfilled God's moral law demonstrating what God intends humans to be and liberating them to become "little Christs."

To understand in a summary way how and why Jesus kept God's law, revealing God as he is and humans as they are and as they were fashioned to be, we shall focus on the Palm Sunday story.

When Jesus entered Jerusalem on the Sunday before the

Passover, he experienced a triumph of person and principle. He discovered firsthand what it means to be the man of the hour, welcomed as a hero, worshiped as a savior. That was part of God's learning firsthand how humans relish other humans ascribing godlike qualities to them. Jesus' handling of this heady experience is one tangible evidence that God was in him. Different translations of the scripture help us to understand the sweeping, deep impact of the Palm Sunday event in the lives of Jesus' contemporaries in Jerusalem. "All the city was moved" (Matthew 21:10 KJV). "All the city was stirred" (RSV). "A shock ran through the whole city" (Philips). "The whole city went wild with excitement" (NEB). "The whole city was thrown into an uproar" (TEV). The Greek verb used in the original text means "to stir, to agitate, to shake violently." Put in contemporary language, the biblical record testifies: "When Jesus entered Jerusalem on the Sunday before the Passover, he stirred the people, agitated the political and religious leaders, and shook the city to its very foundation." It was a grand event: joyous, frenzied, boisterous, pregnant with hope. Indeed, hope was part of the Empire's cultural atmosphere. Under the Emperor Augustus the secular world believed that a golden age was just around the corner. The Jews, chafing under Rome, expected God to deliver them from that tyranny as he had delivered them from the tyranny of the Egyptians. On all sides, expectations ran high.

Before Jesus arrived in the Holy City the populace was expectant. It was also on edge. Social and political tensions had been developing for several decades. Israel despised its status as a Roman province. The Zealots hated the occupying legions as the French would one day, centuries later, hate their Nazi overlords. These Jewish nationalists (insurrectionists) were becoming more bold (irresponsible, according to the Pharisees)—like the French underground in 1943–44—in their subversive deeds of violence against Rome. This growing political conflict was promoted, not only by the Zealots, but also by Jewish collaborators who betrayed their countrymen for a price *and* by the Romans (the ablest "law and order" people in history) who were willing to pay in gold as well as in blood to maintain order in Judea. The political administration in the Judean province also had, in addition to gold and political favors, a full Roman legion for keeping order. Civil revolt anywhere, the Romans judged, could become civil revolt everywhere. These complex tensions, which focused in Jerusalem, antedated Jesus' triumphal entry into the Holy City. The stage was set for violence.

On the particular Sunday Jesus entered Jerusalem the city was more tense than usual. These fresh tensions resulted from thousands of pilgrims crowding into their religious center to celebrate the feast of Passover. There was revelry as well as piety. In some quarters, a Mardi Gras spirit was abroad. Like all crowds this one was unpredictable. So, an already explosive situation became potentially more explosive when Jesus appeared. And the manner and style of Jesus' entry was not calculated to quiet the people in Jerusalem. He did not slip into the Holy City by the back gate. He did not arrive incognito. He came openly and dramatically as Hebrew tradition had promised, deliberately acting out a well-known prophecy (Zechariah 9:9). His entrance created a spectacle. Thousands of people, pouring into the streets, cheered him. He was the man on horseback who would save them from their oppressors, the militant God who would liberate them from the Romans. Jesus' coming to Jerusalem in that high season of religious excitement and political tension rocked the city to its foundations. The crowds demonstrated wildly in support of their Leader. The hosannas rolled out across the Judean hills.

Before the week was over, however, the city's political and religious bureaucracies—allied for the only time in Roman history—playing on the fickle emotions of the unruly crowds, forced Jesus' followers into betrayal, denial, and desertion.

Their personal and corporate sin also rocked Jesus out of historical existence, and unwittingly they gave God opportunity to speak the final word—resurrection. Jesus was dead and buried by late Friday afternoon, barely before the Sabbath began. His mother was numb with grief. His disciples were scattered. One had hanged himself in despair. Another had denied him. No other leader in recorded history had so brief a period of approbation and acclaim. Napoleon had a decade of power—and then another "hundred days" after his escape from Elba in 1815. Franklin D. Roosevelt had twelve years; Andrew Jackson, eight; Winston Churchill, five. Jesus had less than four days!

The people kept asking during that tumultuous week, as people have been asking in every generation since: "Is this man, the Nazarene, the son of Joseph, also the Son of God?" Across the centuries, the church has attempted to answer that question in various ways, each answer, like the question itself, reflecting the culture of a particular era. Here, reflecting our culture, we respond by concentrating on the way Jesus fulfilled God's moral law without violating his personal freedom. Because he, beyond every other person in history, demonstrated the proper balance between freedom and discipline, we can get our bearings from him and understand what he is to us today—and in our freedom, discipline ourselves to walk in his company in the power of God's Spirit.

Jesus fulfilled the moral law of God to the letter and kept its spirit too. In that process, he broke some ecclesiastical and civil laws to teach the Pharisees that the law is not an end in itself; that it exists for the sake of persons; that the law of love is the highest law of all. The Pharisees had forgotten the saving purpose of divine law. They had interpreted and reinterpreted the Ten Commandments to the point where they had produced hundreds of subsidiary laws on how to "keep" the letter of the commandments. For example, one could walk so many feet on the Sabbath without desecrating that holy day. In effect, the Pharisees trivialized God's moral law. They turned a religion of relationships into a religion of mechanics. This crushing legalism spawned self-righteousness. To support their law, the Pharisees sought to limit God's concern to only those persons who kept their law.

Putting the law into proper perspective and reminding the Pharisees that the Sabbath was made for man and not man for the Sabbath, Jesus insisted that the moral law is a concrete expression of God's concern, an act of his grace, and that each commandment carries large promise. His teaching first jarred and then alienated the moralists. It still does. He acknowledged openly the mystery of human existence, the unpredictabilities in human relationships, the ambiguities of human history, the hiddenness as well as the self-disclosure of God, and God's inclusive concern for sinners, Samaritans, Romans, and all people, as well as his concern for the Pharisees themselves. He declared that God is omniscient, omnipotent, *and* all-loving, that humanity and the world are the objects of his saving grace. Jesus fulfilled God's moral law absolutely. We shall examine more precisely how he did that.

The first three commandments have to do with priority-setting, loyalty, and obedience. Consider how Jesus kept them to the letter and breathed a new spirit into them. "I am the Lord your God—" was the benchmark of his life-style. He held to God from Bethlehem to Calvary, from the wilderness to Gethsemane. He set no other gods against Yahweh. He honored his Father at every turn in his human existence. Christians in all eras have recognized Jesus' response as definitive, an example beyond all others. For them, to put God first is to reflect the mind of Jesus, acting out God's justice and claiming his grace.

Jesus—son of Joseph and Mary, truly human, devout Jew—never set himself, his family, his nation, or his race against God. He not only accepted the first commandment as a guide and kept it faithfully; he made it his way of life. The miracle of the Incarnation is not the virgin birth but the Virgin Born, the One who did the will of God from Bethlehem to Golgotha and did not turn aside when the shape of the cross became clear. Jesus did God's will until the breath of life was beaten out of him. It is winsomely and awesomely appealing that he did it with joy in spite of the mental anguish, loneliness of spirit and physical pain engendered in doing it. He did not go to Calvary like a programmed robot or like a galley slave whipped and chained. He laid down his life of his own accord; no one took it from him. He did not go to the cross as one who had failed God and hurt his fellows as Barabbas, freed by the peoples' choice, had done. He went as one who had done his Father's work and shown his fellow humans that they were fashioned for freedom under God's saving authority. He did not go to Calvary cowed by fear of an angry God but crowned with confidence in a loving God.

Fear does play a part in the religious life, often healthily. It always has. In his influential sermon "Sinners in the Hands of an Angry God," Jonathan Edwards used fear to motivate people to do God's will. The fear of the Lord is the beginning of wisdom; it is not the end of it. Martin Luther introduced his explanation of each of the Ten Commandments in the same words: "We should so fear and love God." But the fear of the Lord is not the end of wisdom. Jesus demonstrated that uncalculated love casts out all fear. Paul and Augustine and Luther—like true evangelicals ever since—were liberated from debilitating fear, experienced inner peace, and received power through God's justifying grace. They received and accepted; they did not earn or achieve. And they testified to that with vigor.

Paul Tillich's description of God as the ground of being and Alfred North Whitehead's definition of him as "principle of concretion" have helped critical-minded people to a larger understanding of God in a culture captive to scientism. But Jesus did not argue that God is a cosmic judge bent on punishing lawbreakers, as Jonathan Edwards contended, or as the ground of being as did Paul Tillich, or as a philosophical abstraction as did Alfred North Whitehead. Jesus addressed God intimately, warmly, and confidently, lived with him in a familial relationship, called him Father, and went to Calvary confident that his Father would do what is best for his Son. Jesus' obedience reflected a father-son relationship based on respect, trust, expectation, and love. When he was twelve years old he reminded his human parents, whom he loved dearly, that his first loyalty was to God, his Father, whom he taught was also their Father. On Calvary he prayed, "Father, what you sent me to do has been fully accomplished." Jesus, who held to the first commandment throughout life, held to it also in the hour of his death. His obedience was not the flamboyant gesture of a daring man. It was not a gambler's throw of the dice. It was the act of a Son who trusted his Father.

"Do not treat God's name lightly." Jesus never did. He did not handle it carelessly, never compromised it, never denigrated it in public or in private, never tried to accommodate God's person to contemporary views. Wherever he went, he honored God's name above his own. "Don't call me good," he said, "only God is good." His three dearest friends, accompanying him to Gethsemane, could not watch with him while he struggled desperately to honor God's name to the end. They betrayed God's name simply by falling asleep. Judas, professing loyalty to Jesus, compromised God's name by selling out Jesus for thirty pieces of silver. Simon Peter denied three times that God's name is precious. He went to pieces, not from drink or a centurion's sword against his throat or a governor's threat to crucify him, but from a young servant girl's identifying him as Jesus' disciple. Everyone except Jesus handled God's name carelessly that exhausting night before the crucifixion. He alone kept the second commandment from his first moment of conscious thought to the ninth hour on the cross.

"Remember the Sabbath to keep it holy." Jesus never missed a worship service in the Temple when in Jerusalem or a weekly study session in the synagogue; it was "his custom" to participate. No miserable colds kept him home every week or two and no invitation to go boating on the Lake of Galilee enticed him away from worship and religious study on the weekend. If there had been a *Roman Times,* he would not have substituted its exciting contents for the opportunity to worship God in the company of his fellow humans. Neither comfort nor pleasure nor stimulating secular events and ideas kept him from the appointed religious services in the synagogue and the Temple. It also appears that he tithed. It is clearly documented that he prayed daily. Jesus remembered to worship the living God in the beauty of his holiness and to study God's deeds in Israel's history. He kept the third commandment perfectly.

"Honor your father and mother; respect your traditions." Jesus' relationship with his parents was respectful and loving at all times. He was obedient except when their demands or expectations ran counter to God's claim on him. On those occasions, he did God's bidding, not his parents'. His first loyalty was to God. We recall how he said to his mother after the family visit to Jerusalem: "My first allegiance is to God." At the wedding feast at Cana in Galilee, his mother came to him saying that the host's supply of wine was low. Like most mothers she wanted her son to demonstrate his competence to all who were there. Jesus rebuked her: "I am not here to please you or your friends, but to please God." Jesus' loyalty to God was absolute. But it was this unwavering obedience to God, stronger than his loyalty to his family, that made Jesus a fully responsible son to his earthly parents. From the cross, he climbed above physical pain and spiritual anguish to look clear-eyed on his distraught mother and direct John to care for her. This in-depth respect for his earthly home rested on his absolute respect for his heavenly home. All human relationships are cleansed and renewed when one is in union with God.

This commandment also carries God's directive to remember our religious and civil traditions. Originally, it was addressed to the people of Israel as God's family. Its thrust was corporate, not individual. It was a firm call to keep alive the nation's traditions (chap. 3). Jesus did precisely that. Abraham and Moses and the prophets were in his remembrance daily as he went about doing God's will. He said that plainly: "I have not come to destroy the law and the prophets but to fulfill them." Jesus kept the fourth commandment—respect for parents and traditions—to the letter and enlarged its spirit.

"Do not kill or steal." Neither critic nor follower has ever suggested seriously that Jesus did not keep the letter as well as the spirit of these two commandments. No one has ever suggested that Jesus killed anyone, took anyone's property, or crushed anyone's spirit. During the jagged course of Christian history his followers have killed millions, claiming his sanction for their murderous deeds. They have stolen violently, cleverly, and legally in every generation, often without bothering to claim his sanction. They have crushed millions of human spirits by excluding individuals, social groups, and ethnics from their select gatherings, imprisoning them, ghettoing them, and herding them into concentration camps. Jesus never performed those inhumane deeds. He pushed some private property around on an occasion or two to demonstrate that God's grace is not purchasable. Specifically, he overturned the money changers' tables in the Temple courtyard, jostling a few of the money changers as he went about that task. He drove demons from a deranged man into a herd of swine. That one-time disregard for property rights was deliberate; he was demonstrating concretely that persons are more precious to God than possessions. But Jesus never raised a hand or spoke a word that brought permanent harm or injury or death to any human being.

"Do not commit adultery." Jesus fulfilled this law to the letter and breathed into it a new spirit. If he were, as the Scriptures reveal and the church teaches and I believe, bone of our bone and flesh of our flesh, then he experienced every natural passion. To be wholesomely attacted to women and to attract them in turn were strands in Jesus' earthly person. He did not denigrate marriage as a segment of his church would do after the tenth century by linking celibacy to ordination. He blessed the marriage at Cana; on every occasion he honored marriage and fostered parental responsibility. But his primary obligation to God precluded his entering into this holy human relationship, even as parental and vocational commitments of others in succeeding generations have persuaded them, in their freedom, to forego marriage.

Jesus also enlarged this commandment by being the most radical initiator of women's and children's rights in recorded history. The current Equal Rights Amendment to our Constitution reflects only a fraction of his sweeping addressment to human rights for women—and for children too. This is remarkable because he lived in a social order that regarded women as chattels and gave each father the power of life and death over his children.[2] He accepted Mary and Martha (respectable in any community), Mary Magdalene (not respectable in her community), his mother (honored by the church), and women everywhere as equals with men in the family of God. He provided the reason for Paul to argue that, as there is neither male nor female in God's kingdom, men and women are equal in God's family.

Paul did not get altogether free of Judaism and Hellenistic culture. Consequently, his understanding of female rights in marriage is decidedly less than Jesus' teaching on *human* dignity. But Paul did enunciate the principle on which equality between the sexes rests and expressed its spirit: "Husbands love your wives as Christ also loved the church." The church across the centuries forgot the principle and the spirit. Consequently, it failed Christ miserably on this pivotal human issue, as it has failed him often on the issues of social justice, war, peace, stewardship, and social ministry. Nonetheless, Jesus' attitude toward and teaching about women and children is clear: he accepted men and women and children as persons equal in the family of God, each to be understood and related to as a person. He declared that those who harmed or used children to their own advantage would come to a bad end; it would be better for anyone who harms a little child if a large millstone were tied around his neck and he were thrown in the sea (see Luke 17:2). Jesus kept the eighth commandment to the letter. Miraculously, he enlarged its spirit incomparably.

"Do not bear false witness." It is staggering to reflect how Jesus always told the truth. It is awesome to study how he always did it in love. There is no comparison between his truth-telling and ours either in boldness or compassion. He told the religious leaders of his day that they were rotten inside—"whited sepulchers." The difference between Jesus' truth-telling and ours is larger than the difference between a Rembrandt painting and a Rockwell watercolor, between Beethoven's Ninth Symphony and Irving Berlin's "White Christmas." The difference is both qualitative and quantitative. Jesus not only told the whole truth; he always spoke it in love.

Even as Jesus told the truth to and about persons, he also told the truth about God. What is God like? we ask. Jesus teaches that God is like a shepherd who seeks one lost sheep, a woman who searches for a single lost coin, a father who waits to welcome home his wayward son (Luke 15). Jesus assures us that God is like the prodigal's father; that God loves us exactly as we are, wherever we are, in whatever condition we are (the son forgot his father for a season, but the father never forgot his son); that God's love is structured by his righteousness (the son could come home anytime he chose, on the father's terms); that God saves us through our freedom without violating that freedom and in the process lifts us to a higher kind of freedom (the son asked for his inheritance, the father gave it, and when the son came to his senses and returned home, he was received fully). Jesus spoke the whole truth about God.

"Do not covet." Jesus coveted only one thing! He wanted inordinately to do God's will. "I must do the works of him who sent me." "Blessed are they who hunger and thirst after righteousness." That is the experiential side of the first commandment. When one's hunger for God's righteousness is dominant, then all human desires fall into place. It is as elemental as that.

Obedient to the whole law of God, Jesus fulfilled it perfectly in letter and in spirit. For him the law was not a legalistic device to preserve the "righteous" man from sin and the corrupting influence of sinners in society. In Jesus' redemptive hands, the law was not only God's judgment but equally his grace. By the law, as Jesus understood and recast it (Matthew 5), he pursued and sought out sinners (Zacchaeus—"I am coming to your house today"), forgave sinners and gave them a new model for the good life and the power to live it (the woman taken in adultery), and always accepted sinners as persons, cultivating them for the Kingdom (the rich young ruler, the woman at the well).

So, Jesus—in perfect fulfillment of the law, while always befriending those outside the law—alienated those who lived narrowly within the letter of the law. They would not accept his higher truth that God intended his law to reach out in love to all persons. To preserve the integrity of that law as they understood it, they killed Jesus, thus sacrificing one man in order, as they held in their blindness, to save the whole nation from corruption. Far beyond anything we can possibly do, Jesus fulfilled the law. He was put to death precisely because he was not satisfied to obey the law in the narrow, legalistic way of the Pharisees. He obeyed God's law fully and by his death liberates all responsive persons to accept the law of perfect love, covered always by God's grace. Christ died to free us from sin. No one, I think, has said this better than Martin Luther in his explanation of the second article of the Apostles' Creed, his concise declaration that balances the historical and the existential: "The Lord Jesus Christ has redeemed me, a lost and condemned person. He has freed me from sin, death, and the power of the devil—not with silver or gold, but with his holy and precious blood and his innocent suffering and death."[3]

Across the centuries, millions of Christians have recognized that only Jesus fulfilled God's moral law and that God's saving grace is wrapped up in that deed. But that truth-event repels many. Nietzsche would have none of it. Nor would Bertrand Russell. Neither would the poet Swinburne, who sneered at Jesus:

> Thou hast conquered, O pale Galilean;
> the world has grown gray from thy breath.

Jesus has also attracted many only to have them defect when the going got rough. But millions of others, attracted to Jesus, have held to his way. Loved by him, they have loved him in return. Paul and Augustine, Francis of Assisi and Joan d'Arc, John Huss and Savonarola, John Wesley and George Fox, John Milton and Jonathan Edwards, Friedrich Schliermacher and Robert Browning, Abraham Lincoln and Woodrow Wilson, William Temple and Reinhold Niebuhr—and thousands of millions like you and me across a hundred generations of people who have lived and died in the faith.

In fulfilling God's law, Jesus effected the rescue of lost persons and summarized the law, the prophets, and the gospel: "Love God with your whole being and your neighbor as you love yourself." Bone of our bone, sinew of our sinew, flesh of our flesh—yet very God of very God—Jesus assures us by his acceptance and his forgiveness that we can grow in keeping God's law. He promises that we can live life abundantly here if we follow him and become whole when we meet him face to face.

Yet we fumble and falter and fail. When we reflect on what obedience to God cost Jesus—hatred, desertion, betrayal, rejection, crucifixion—our common sense, conformism, and cowardice hold us back. We doubt that his grace is sufficient for us. Paul, experiencing this tension between human grandeur and misery, described the true Christian stance:

> Does this mean that what is good caused my death? By no means! It was sin that did it; by using what is good, sin brought death to me, in order that its true nature as sin might be revealed. And so, by means of the commandment sin is shown to be even more terribly sinful.
>
> We know that the Law is spiritual; but I am mortal man, sold as a slave to sin. I do not understand what I do; for I don't do what I would like to do, but instead I do what I hate. Since what I do is what I don't want to do, this shows that I agree that the Law is right. So I am not really the one who does this thing; rather it is the sin that lives in me. I know that good does not live in me—that is, in my human nature. For even though the desire to do good is in me, I am not able to do it. I don't do the good I want to do; instead, I do the evil that I do not want to do. If I do what I don't want to do, this means that no longer am I the one who does it; instead, it is the sin that lives in me.
>
> So I find that this law is at work: when I want to do what is good, what is evil is the only choice I have. My inner being delights in the law of God. But I see a different law at work in my body—a law that fights against the law which my mind approves of. It makes me a prisoner to the law of sin which is at work in my body. What an unhappy man I am! Who will rescue me from this body that is taking me to death? Thanks be to God, who does this through our Lord Jesus Christ! (Romans 7:13-25 TEV)

We do not yet know what we shall be in Christ or what that "weight of glory" entails, but experiencing his deliverance from bondage now, we receive a larger freedom to affirm those disciplines without which the good life is impossible and apart from which we shall not work long nor well for a just society here. Christ enables us to get freedom and discipline into a working balance. And we, surprised by joy, discover anew that we *are* fashioned for freedom and that in Christ we can learn to exercise it responsibly.

This is the new morality for our bruised, bleeding, broken world.

AppenÒix

Study groups may want to use some of these questions to stimulate discussion.

I. ON FREEDOM AND DISCIPLINE

1. What do the words *freedom* and *discipline* mean to you? Check the several definitions in a good dictionary like *Webster's New International Dictionary*, second edition.
2. How does self-discipline protect your personal freedom? The liberties of others?
3. What do you mean when you use the words *moral, immoral, amoral*? Do you have a fixed point of moral reference for judging events, ideas, and persons? Does it strengthen your moral sense to tackle each ethical decision *de novo* (from scratch)?
4. Liberal democracy (legally guaranteed individual liberties in an ordered, just society) was envisioned in America and framed for a rural citizenry of three million people scattered along the Atlantic seaboard. Can that concept and political system survive in the radically different historical setting and culture of 1980? Should we work to keep it? Why? Do you prize the individual rights that are guaranteed in the first ten amendments to the Constitution: (a) for yourself and (b) for others, especially those who disagree with you? Be specific.

5. Does biblical Christianity (Old and New Testament) address social and political institutions as well as individuals and families? Discuss. Do you trust (a) political leaders? (b) business people? (c) lawyers? (d) doctors? (e) clergy? (f) your mate? (g) your children? (h) a friend or two?
6. America may be the only major power presently committed to liberal democracy. Many of our citizens and millions in other nations judge that America is giving up on liberal democracy (individual liberties) and is moving inexorably into totalitarian democracy. What do you think? Does this issue concern you?
7. If you were forced to choose, would you elect to live in a nation with legal guarantees of individual liberties that experiences periodic economic fluctuations and social inequities, or would you prefer to live in a nation that guarantees personal security but allows few individual liberties? Broadly, liberal democracy provides the first choice; totalitarian democracy and state socialism the second. Our Constitution allows either choice to be made peaceably. Discuss.

II. ON AUTHORITY, FREEDOM, AND DISCIPLINE

1. Identify and discuss the difference between authority and authoritarianism. Do you believe God is (a) arbitrary? (b) capricious? (c) just? (d) loving? (e) concerned about you? Be specific.
2. Serious Christians seek to understand the authority of God and struggle to accept it. Does this struggle (a) delimit your freedom? (b) diminish your dignity? (c) frustrate you? (d) anger you? Discuss. Read the book of Jeremiah for perspective on one man's struggle to accept God's authority in his life.
3. Discuss the concept of "obedience in freedom" in biblical context. Relate this concept to Jesus' call (a) to take up your cross daily, (b) to his declaration that "the straight gate and narrow way" lead to freedom, (c) to his promise that abundant life is God's gift to his disciplined followers.
4. Do you pit your mate, child, money, success, security, class, race, nation against the true God? Discuss. How do you cope with the calls of the false gods in our technological-urban-bureaucratic mass culture?
5. Discuss human pride in (a) secular terms, (b) biblical terms.

6. Is any human conscience trustworthy? What did Martin Luther mean when he declared that his conscience was "captive to the Word of God"? Was he appealing to an authority outside himself? Do you ever make an appeal like that?
7. What does the phrase "the imperial presidency" mean? Is the concentration of power in the president's office inevitable in our technological-bureaucratic government? Responsible citizenship requires that we understand our political traditions. Discuss ways that you and others can enlarge your knowledge, appreciation, and understanding of the political traditions that shaped our nation.
8. Do you accept Jesus' declaration that those who love him will do his commandments? Examine yourself on your response to his love in relating to (a) mate, (b) child, (c) friend, (d) fellow workers, (e) people of other classes, races, nations.
9. Do you regard corporate worship as an elective or a required course in your Christian growth?
10. Can anyone know and follow Christ outside the church? Discuss.

III. WHERE RESPONSIBLE RELATIONSHIPS BEGIN

1. There has always been a degree of tension between the generations. Is this tension deeper today? What does the term "generation gap" mean to you?
2. Do you respect your parents? Why? Where do you think your parents help(ed) and support(ed) you? Hurt and put you down? As a parent, do you rear your children with the same philosophy your parents used in rearing you? What is different in your parental style?
3. Do you provoke your children to anger by (a) not listening to them? (b) declining to see their points of view? (c) not discussing events, persons, and ideas with them? (d) not showing affection? (e) not disciplining them responsibly? (f) not giving them the freedom to make mistakes?
4. Define and discuss the word *tradition* in these contexts: (a) religious, (b) political, (c) economic, (d) social, (e) military, (f) academic. Are there good and bad traditions? Discuss concretely.

5. From your experience, would you conclude that most parents like as well as love their children? Do most children like as well as love their parents?
6. Is it ever right to tell an untruth? Discuss, using concrete examples from specific situations.
7. Do you think it is possible to discern the whole truth in any situation or about any person or about yourself?
8. Do you think it is possible to find some good in every person and in every historical situation? What does the hymn line "Greater good because of evil" mean ("There's a Wideness in God's Mercy," verse 7)?
9. Discerning the truth and telling it causes trouble. Agree? Disagree? Discuss concretely.
10. Have you ever prayed specifically for someone who has been mean to you? For an enemy? For another nation that was threatening your nation?

IV. FASHIONING A STABLE SOCIETY

1. Which acts among the following, if any, violate the commandment against killing: (a) killing in self-defense? (b) a war to protect one's shores, society, way of life? (c) capital punishment? (d) police action against a deranged killer? (e) suicide? (f) euthanasia? (g) abortion? (h) drinking, plus an act of violence with an auto, gun, blunt object, or fist that results in death?
2. How can one keep the fifth commandment when—as a counselor, doctor, police officer, soldier, or fire fighter—one is forced to decide directly or indirectly which of two lives shall be preserved or—as a citizen or political leader—one must decide which of several nations shall be attacked or counterattacked or supported?
3. What does "the right to life" mean (a) biblically? (b) existentially? (c) socially? (d) legally? Consider next "the right to die" in the same contexts. Presently, California is the only state in the Union with "a right to die" law. Should such a law be enacted in all the states?
4. A recent Columbia University study revealed that an American from infancy to age eighteen will witness more than thirteen hundred murders in television viewing. Does this, as the study suggests, create mass fear in our society? Discuss.
5. We agree that taking another person's wallet or bicycle or auto is

stealing. Identify other ways in which we and others steal personally and corporately in a world of rapidly dwindling resources. Discuss.

6. Did the colonizers of America (Spanish, French, Dutch, and English) steal the land from the Indians? Did the American revolutionaries steal when they confiscated the property of the Loyalists? Did the Southern aristocracy steal from the blacks when they built the Southern economy on slave labor? Did the American government steal the Southwest from Mexico? Did the blacks steal when they looted Watts, Newark, Washington, and Detroit? Did students steal when they destroyed property on college campuses in the 1960s? Do Americans steal when they overeat, overdrink, and overconsume in a world in which a third of the inhabitants can barely exist and millions die?

7. The seventh commandment does not speak to or about premarital sex between consenting adults. What is your judgment on premarital sex—religiously, medically, emotionally?

8. Is extramarital sex ever therapeutic? Discuss.

9. There are many causes of marital infidelity in American society. Should these breakdowns in relationships end automatically in divorce for all Christian couples? Do you think premarriage, marriage, and family counseling can be helpful? Discuss.

10. In this chapter, we pointed to a new openness in American society to the homosexual life-style. In what way(s) do you think the church can (should) be more open? Do you consider homosexuality to be an acceptable life-style among consenting adults or an emotional immaturity to be treated? Should the church ordain men and women who—otherwise qualified—identify themselves as confirmed and practicing homosexuals?

V. ON BEING FREE TO APPRECIATE OTHERS

1. Envy, we said, is the personal problem Christians do not talk about. Discuss.

2. We have argued that pride and envy are mates and that their offspring are covetousness, greed, and jealousy. Discuss.

3. Do you envy anyone? Be as honest as you can. Talk it out if you judge that doing so will be a wholesome experience.

4. Do you believe that God can cleanse your conscious and unconscious desires? Do you ever pray: "Create in me a clean heart"? If so, what do you expect through that prayer?

5. How do affluence and technology sustain and spread envy?
6. Distinguish between (a) normal jealousy and neurotic jealousy, (b) a balanced desire for material comforts and outright greed, (c) living by conscience rather than by convenience. Take a fresh look at the prodigal's brother (Luke 15:21-30). What was his basic fault?
7. What should we covet (want inordinately) as Christians? Do you experience moments when you hunger and thirst after righteousness? When? Where? Do you cultivate this fleeting desire? How? Is this hunger stronger than it was five, ten, twenty, forty years ago? Has it influenced your thinking, speaking, and acting? How?
8. In your daily work, do you see yourself as seeking to be moral in an immoral society? Be specific.

VI. HOW ONE MAN GOT FREEDOM AND DISCIPLINE IN BALANCE

1. Read, integrate, and discuss the gospel accounts of Jesus' last week. (Matthew 26–28; Mark: 14–16; Luke: 22–24; John: 13–21).
2. Do you consider that Jesus was as human as you biologically, intellectually, emotionally, volitionally? Do you ever feel that he had the edge on you—that he was superhuman?
3. What do the scriptures mean when they declare that Jesus fulfilled the moral law of God?
4. What does salvation mean to you? Justification through faith? The "mind of Christ" in you? Growth in grace? Christ "appealing by you"?
5. What, in your situation, is the cost of Christian stewardship?
6. Was Jesus programmed for Calvary? Could he have avoided the Cross? Discuss.
7. Do you think Jesus enjoyed living in this world? Discuss.
8. How do you understand (a) Jesus' Gethsemane prayer, "If it be possible—" and (b) Jesus' cry of dereliction, "My God, why have you forsaken me?"
9. What does Christ's resurrection mean to you? Do you view it as an event? An experience? Both?
10. Do you expect, in the presence of Christ (when you die in the faith), to be made a whole person?

NOTES

PREFACE

1. For a detailed discussion, see Karl Menninger, *Whatever Became of Sin?* (New York: Hawthorn Books, 1973), and Reinhold Niebuhr, *The Nature and Destiny of Man* (New York: Macmillan, 1944), vol. 1. For a brief discussion, see D. R. Davies, *Down Peacock's Feathers* (New York: Macmillan, 1947), chaps. 2-5.
2. Lillian Hellman, *Scoundrel Time* (Boston: Little, Brown, 1976).
3. For the full text, see Theodore G. Tappert, ed., *Selected Writings of Martin Luther, 1520-1533* (Philadelphia: Fortress Press, 1967), pp. 5-53. Luther's "two propositions," widely quoted over the centuries, are these:

> A Christian is a perfectly free lord of all, subject to none.
> A Christian is a perfectly dutiful servant of all, subject to all.

I. ON FREEDOM AND DISCIPLINE

1. *New York Times Book Review*, February 20, 1977, pp. 1, 16.
2. Walker Percy, *Lancelot* (New York: Farrar, Strauss & Giroux), p. 239. See also B. F. Skinner, *Beyond Freedom and Dignity* (New York: Macmillan, 1972), who argues that society must surrender not only the rhetoric of freedom but all hope for it and that it must systematically condition human beings to live responsibly in a technological society.

3. Sydney E. Ahlstrom, *A Religious History of the American People* (New Haven: Yale University Press, 1972), p. 1094.

4. Thomas Lockman, *Invisible Religion* (New York, Macmillan, 1967), pp. 97-99. The 1976-77 TV series "Mary Hartman, Mary Hartman" is a farce on this reality.

5. Alistair Cooke, *America* (New York: Knopf, 1974), pp. 387-88.

6. Harry Emerson Fosdick, *What Is Vital in Religion?* (New York: Harper, 1955), p. 165.

7. *World Issues,* December, 1976, p. 14. See also Kai T. Erikson, *Everything in Its Path* (New York: Simon & Schuster, 1977), for a sociological study of morality in the coal industry in West Virginia.

8. John Neuhaus, *Time Toward Home* (New York: The Seabury Press, 1976), p. 19. This brilliant discussion of biblical and civil religion in America deserves careful reading in ecclesiastical, political, and academic circles. See also Martin E. Marty, *Righteous Empire* (New York: Harper, 1969).

9. See Henry Fairlee, *The Politics of Promise* (New York: Harper, 1974), for an insightful discussion of this issue.

10. W. E. Woodyard, *Strangers and Exiles* (New York: Harper, 1974), p. 34.

11. See William Stringfellow and Anthony Towne, *The Death and Life of Bishop Pike* (New York: Harper, 1976), and Judith Rossman, *Looking for Mr. Goodbar* (New York: Simon & Schuster, 1975), for poignant examples of this deep yearning set in fact and in fiction.

12. Philip Slater, *The Pursuit of Loneliness: American Culture at the Breaking Point* (Boston: Beacon Press, 1970).

13. Rollo May, *Love and Will* (New York: W. W. Norton, 1969), p. 139.

14. *Washington Watch,* vol. 4, no. 18.

15. *Time,* May 3, 1976, p. 65.

16. *The Lutheran,* June 2, 1976.

17. *Intelligencer-Journal* (Lancaster, Pa.), June 4, 1976. The italics are mine.

18. Sloan Wilson, *What Shall We Wear to This Party?* (New York: Simon & Schuster, 1976).

19. Richard M. Heiber, *The American Idea of Success* (New York: McGraw-Hill, 1971), especially chaps. 10-18.

20. *World Issues,* p. 15.

21. John E. Biersdorf, *Hunger for Experience* (New York: The Seabury Press, 1976), especially pp. 12-22.

22. For an in-depth study, see Godfrey Hodgson, *America in Our Time* (Garden City, N. Y.: Doubleday).

II. ON AUTHORITY, FREEDOM, AND DISCIPLINE

1. Rap Brown's declaration that "violence is as American as apple pie" is historically accurate. See Richard Hofstadter and Michael Wallace, eds., *American Violence: A Documentary History* (New York: Knopf, 1970).

2. Bacon's Rebellion, 1670, was an armed revolt of frontier farmers in Virginia against the merchants and planters on the Atlantic seaboard.

3. Henry Steele Commager, *The American Mind* (New Haven: Yale University Press, 1959), p. 410.

4. See Wallace E. Fisher, *Politics, Poker, and Piety* (Nashville: Abingdon, 1972), chaps. 1, 4.

5. Ann and Barry Ulanov, *Religion and the Unconscious* (Philadelphia: Westminster Press, 1975), p. 216.

6. See Barbara Tuchman, *Proud Tower* (New York: Macmillan, 1972), for a brilliant analysis of the road to World War I and commentary on the human sin of pride and its far-reaching social consequences.

7. See Mary Alice Kellogg, "Washington's Star Stargazer," *New York Times Magazine*, January 16, 1977, for a report on American legislators' use of astrology.

8. See Arthur M. Schlesinger, Jr., *The Imperial Presidency* (New York: Macmillan, 1972), for a detailed, documented study of this crucial change in American political life. See also David Halberstam, *The Best and the Brightest* (New York: Random House, 1969), for a documented study on the inadequacies of "specialists" in a political administration.

9. See C. P. Snow, *Science and Government* (Cambridge: Harvard University Press, 1961) for a sobering study on this aspect of politics and technology.

10. Fairlee, *The Politics of Promise*, chap. 1.

11. Lukas Vischer, *Tithing in the Early Church*, trans. Robert C. Schultz (Philadelphia: Fortress Press, 1966), p. 10.

12. President Carter's record is not yet in.

13. See, as one example, Richard Klinger's *Simple Justice* (New York: Knopf, 1976), a detailed account of black America's struggle for equality under the law. This work may become a classic. See also John Kenneth Galbraith, *The Affluent Society*, 3rd ed. rev. (New York: Houghton Mifflin, 1976), named by the American Library Associa-

tion as one of the ten most influential books on modern opinion. See also Sheldon Novick, *The Electric War: The Fight Over Nuclear Power* (San Francisco: Sierra Club Books, 1976), a partisan but solid corrective.

14. Spencer Marsh, *God, Man, and Archie Bunker* (New York: Harper, 1974), p. 34.

15. Leslie Farber, *Lying, Despair, Jealousy, Envy, Sex, Suicide, Drugs, and the Good Life* (New York: Basic Books, 1976), p. 119. Farber, writing on our addictive society, states that "the medical profession and the pharmaceutical industry keep offering and prescribing more non-narcotic drugs 'to will away the unhappiness that comes from willing ourselves to be happy.' "

16. Ferdinand Hahn, *The Worship of the Early Church*, trans. David E. Greer, ed. John Reuman (Philadelphia: Fortress Press, 1971), p. 21. See also Joachim Jeremias, *The Central Message of the New Testament* (New York: Scribner's, 1965).

17. Hahn, *Worship of the Early Church*, pp. 22-23; Jeremias, *Central Message*, pp. 17-21.

18. See Herbert Benson, *The Relaxation Response* (New York: Harper, 1975).

19. James Carroll, *The Winter Name of God* (New York: Sheed & Ward, 1975), p. 166.

III. WHERE RESPONSIBLE RELATIONSHIPS BEGIN

1. See Robert Michaelson, *Piety in the Public School* (New York: Macmillan, 1970). This carefully researched study enables one to understand how and why Americans viewed public education as a sacred democratic institution, 1790–1950.

2. Originally, this commandment appears to have been addressed also to *adult* children, admonishing them not to expose their aged and ill parents to wild animals and the elements, as surrounding societies did. See J. J. Stamm and M. E. Andren, *The Ten Commandments in Recent Research* (London: SCM Press, 1967).

3. Gibson Winter, *Being Free: Reflections on America's Cultural Revolution* (New York: Macmillan, 1970), p. 140.

4. The best American work on this, I think, remains H. Richard Niebuhr's *Christ and Culture* (New York: Harper, 1951). Lay leaders, as well as clergy, should read and discuss this seminal study.

5. Some informed estimates claim that one million or more children are abused physically by parents every year. In my counseling experience, this vicious but emotionally complex and tragic problem comes up too frequently.
6. See Carl Rogers, *On Personal Power: Inner Strength and Its Revolutionary Impact* (New York: Delacorte Press, 1977), especially pp. 29-42.
7. See Gloria Emerson, *Winners And Losers: Battles, Retreats, Gains, Losses and Ruins from a Long War* (New York: Random House, 1976). To date, this is *the* account of the tragedy of the Vietnam War. Every serious citizen should read the book.

IV. FASHIONING A STABLE SOCIETY

1. This part of the litany was brought to my attention by one of the readers of this manuscript, Hugo Eskildson. A fuller treatment of this crucial distinction is presented in the rest of this chapter. See also Wallace E. Fisher, *A New Climate for Stewardship* (Nashville: Abingdon, 1976), chaps. 1-3.
2. Anonymous.
3. John Ellis, *The Social History of the Machine Gun* (New York: Pantheon Books, 1975), provides a sobering view of technology *against* humanity.
4. See Fisher, *Politics, Poker, Piety,* chap. 1.
5. See Fisher, *New Climate,* chap. 1.
6. *Ibid.,* especially chaps. 2, 4.
7. See Robert Heilbroner, *Between Capitalism and Socialism* (New York: Random House, 1970), on the "predicted" breakdown of capitalism.
8. *The Cambridge Bible Commentary,* s. v. "Deuteronomy."
9. Some adults, particularly clergy and secular counselors, will find another early church father's views interesting and forthright: Tertullian, *Treatises on Marriage and Remarriage* (Westminster, Md.: The Newman Press). Compare his view on sex with Augustine's, p. 40.
10. Sydney E. Ahlstrom, "The Radical Turn in Theology and Ethics: Why It Occurred in the 1960s," *The Annals of the American Academy of Political and Social Science,* 387, 3.
11. See Vance Packard, *The Sexual Wilderness* (New York: David McKay Co., 1968), especially chaps. 2, 3, and 4.
12. May, *Love and Will,* pp. 67-72.

13. "The New Feminism," *Saturday Review*, February 21, 1970, pp. 29-30. Other feminists have also made this observation over the years.

14. May, *Love and Will*, p. 58.

15. See Joseph Fletcher, *Situation Ethics: The New Morality* (Philadelphia: Westminster Press, 1966).

16. See Joseph Fletcher, *Moral Responsibility: Situation Ethics at Work* (Philadelphia: Westminster Press, 1967), chap. 5; and *Storm Over Ethics* (Philadelphia: United Church Press, 1976), especially chaps. 2, 4, 5.

17. *Saturday Review*, August 7, 1976, p. 38.

18. My own professional judgment is that homosexuality is an immaturity to be treated.

19. May, *Love and Will*, pp. 45, 61.

20. Farber, *Lying, Despair, Jealousy*, pp. 123-45.

21. *New York Times Book Review*, May 9, 1976.

22. Howard J. Clinebell and Charlotte Clinebell, *The Intimate Marriage* (New York: Harper, 1976), is a solid resource book for serious-minded couples.

V. ON BEING FREE TO APPRECIATE OTHERS

1. Farber, *Lying, Despair, Jealousy*, p. 36.

2. See Philip M. Stern, *The Oppenheimer Case: Security on Trial* (New York: Harper, 1969). Concerning Oppenheimer's trial, David Lilienthal said, "There hasn't been a proceeding like this since the Spanish Inquisition."

3. Farber, *Lying, Despair, Jealousy*, pp. 36-37.

4. See Carl Bernstein and Bob Woodward, *All the President's Men* (New York: Simon & Schuster, 1974); Doris Kearns, *Lyndon Johnson and the American Dream* (New York: Harper, 1976); Eric F. Goldman, *The Tragedy of Lyndon Johnson* (New York: Knopf, 1968); and David Abrahamsen, *Nixon Against Nixon: An Emotional Tragedy* (New York: Farrar, Strauss & Giroux), a psychobiography, solidly done. Nonetheless, my graduate training in history makes me cautious in accepting this kind of "history." It provides valuable insights, but it must be balanced by factual accounts of events that are damning enough.

5. Police, fire fighters, workers in the Disease Control Center in

Atlanta, military personnel, and many others risk life and limb daily in behalf of others.

6. Blaise Pascal, *Pensees* (New York: Dutton, 1965), p. 65.

VI. HOW ONE MAN GOT DISCIPLINE AND FREEDOM IN BALANCE

1. The Atonement—"Jesus died for our sins"—is a reality that outruns our theologies, hymns, prayers, and preaching. In speaking here about Jesus' fulfilling God's law, we are considering only one significant strand in God's saving work in Christ.

2. John Thompson, *Jesus' Audience* (New York: Herder and Herder, 1975), chap. 2.

3. Luther's explanation, in part, of the second article of the Apostles' Creed on the person and work of Christ. See any of the several editions of Luther's *Small Catechism*.